Make the Noise Go Away

Make the Noise Go Away

The Power of an Effective Second-in-Command

by
Larry G. Linne
with
Ken Koller

Foreword by Ken Blanchard

iUniverse, Inc.
Bloomington

iUniverse Star
an iUniverse, Inc. imprint

iUniverse books may be ordered through booksellers or by contacting:

iUniverse
1663 Liberty Drive
Bloomington, IN 47403
www.iuniverse.com
1-800-Authors (1-800-288-4677)

ISBN: 978-1-936236-73-2 (sc)
ISBN: 978-1-936236-74-9 (e)

Library of Congress Control Number: 2011908300

Printed in the United States of America

iUniverse rev. date: 6/7/2011

Contents

Foreword i

Acknowledgments iii

Introduction v

Chapter 1 The Noise 1

Chapter 2 The Power of an Effective Second-in-Command 3

Chapter 3 Principles That Make the Noise Go Away 8

Chapter 4 Upward Communication 11

Chapter 5 A Problem Solver 18

Chapter 6 Doing What I Enjoy and What I Do Best 26

Chapter 7 Keeping Priorities 31

Chapter 8 Aligning with Owner Values 37

Chapter 9 Reflecting over Coffee 45

Chapter 10 Losing Sleep 47

Chapter 11 Making the Company Look Good 51

Chapter 12 Spending Time with Clients 58

Chapter 13 The Second-in-Command's Keys to Success 63

Chapter 14 The First-in-Command's Keys to Success 66

Chapter 15 Leading Versus Doing 69

Chapter 16 Bringing New Ideas 73

Chapter 17 Bringing Results 78

Chapter 18 Hiring an Effective Second-in-Command 86

Chapter 19 The Awakening 94

Epilogue The Rest of the Story 101

Foreword

Noise surrounds me. Given the fact that I've never heard a bad idea, implementation hasn't always been my strength. A lot of people say that I've been very successful in my life. Let me reword that: *we've* been very successful. If it weren't for the talented second-in-commands surrounding me, I would have gone down a long time ago. These people have been able to take my visions and bring them alive, whether it's been writing projects or building the The Ken Blanchard Companies® from scratch into a global leader in training and development. That is why I'm so excited to introduce *Make the Noise Go Away: The Power of an Effective Second-in-Command*—because Larry Linne has put into words what I've discovered through experience.

If you're an entrepreneur, a CEO, or a big thinker of any kind, the noise around you can make your effectiveness plummet. Without a strong second-in-command, you'll be doing work in the low priority C piles, letting the high priority A piles languish, and probably losing sleep. Larry Linne's ideas will give you clarity on the noise so that you can make the right decisions and sleep better at night. If you're a second-in-command, this book will help you understand the critical role you play in any success story. You'll discover the real concerns of your first-in-command and acquire the tools you need to resolve those concerns.

My wife, Margie, learned about the power of second-in-commands many years ago when she was on speaking program with author and teacher Rosabeth Moss Kanter. While sharing a cab on the way to the airport, Rosabeth mentioned an article to Margie and promised to send it to her. Three days later, Margie had the book in her hands. She was blown away that someone as busy as Rosabeth could follow through that quickly. The next time she saw Rosabeth, Margie related her astonished admiration. Rosabeth smiled and said, "I figured out how to be a great wife, mother, professor, and friend. It's a staff of three or four." Shortly after that Margie put an ad in the newspaper that essentially said "busy executive looking for a wife." She hired a personal assistant—a second-in-command—and it revolutionized her effectiveness.

I have to add that Margie has probably been the best second-in-command of my life, and I've probably been her best second-in-command. When you can play that role for each other, you've got a great marriage.

Whether you're a first-in-command in overwhelm or a second-in-command wondering how you can be more effective, read this book. You'll both sleep better at night.

—Ken Blanchard,
coauthor of *The One Minute Manager*®
and *Leading at a Higher Level*

Acknowledgments

When you start a book you think you can do it yourself. Then you realize you can't write. Then you realize you have a family and a job. Then you realize you can't do this alone. So, though thank you is never enough, it is all I have. I hope millions of people read this book—not necessarily so I sell this book, but because I want to show my appreciation to these people.

To my girls, Debi, Tiffany, Wen Jun, Macie, Avree, and Lia, thank you for teaching me about family. Ken, your project management skills and experiences have been the keys to getting this book written. You are a great partner. Bill Golden, the model first-in-command, it wouldn't have happened without you challenging me and teaching me. Roger Sitkins, I gave the world a little touch of you in this book. You need to write the next one. Thanks for the opportunity and the opportunities. Dan Taylor, you are an inspiration, and you helped me create my brand. Larry, Jerry, and Joe, thanks for the trust, respect, classroom, and the experiences. Effective second-in-command class attendees, thanks for the stories. Sitkins International, thanks for not letting me quit this project. Steve L., thanks for the location idea. Steve and Duane, *Make The Noise Go Away* would have been something else without you. Dan Sullivan, the Strategic Coach Program is the best in the world because it lifted the glass ceiling from my roof. Mr. Blanchard, you are an answered prayer. I could never thank you enough. Finally, my God has given me gifts I don't understand. Thank you for giving me those gifts and for not taking those gifts from me when I don't use them to the fullest!

Introduction

"I became an entrepreneur because I wanted to have freedom in my life. I wanted financial freedom and time freedom. Now that I own the business, I have neither. I don't own this business—this business owns me!" These were the words of one of my clients during a consulting session a few years ago.

This transition from owning to being owned is very typical of many chief executive officers, presidents, business leaders, and entrepreneurs. They get into business with dreams of great freedom but end up with a lot of things running through their heads day and night. This is what many of those CEOs or first-in-commands call "noise."

I was a second-in-command early in my business career and was fortunate enough to figure out how to make the noise go away for my first-in-command. After we experienced this success, many of my first-in-command's friends hired me to help them make the noise go away by training them and their second-in-commands. I continued my career as a second-in-command for three CEOs over a fifteen-year period. All three have been very successful. During that time period I developed eleven principles to make the noise go away for a first-in-command. Since then I have continued to work as a consultant with hundreds of first- and second-in-command executives to help them make the noise go away.

When I became a first-in-command I implemented the strategies from a different perspective than before. This perspective has helped me to refine the principles to help the first- and second-in-command make the noise go away.

I decided to write this book because the demand for my

principles has become so great that I can't get to all the clients who are asking for help.

So what is the "noise"?

Over the past fifteen years of coaching first- and second-in–commands I've seen the noise come in numerous forms. A first-in-command who has a lot of noise might:

- Feel anxiety and doubt about the business
- Receive a lot of feedback that his or her new ideas are driving the company crazy
- Have low trust that things will be accomplished
- Be the only person who brings value to outside relationships
- Feel the need to do everything himself or herself
- Feel as if he or she is the only one in the business losing sleep
- Check up on every detail of the business because he or she doesn't know what is going on
- Be so busy doing everything but not have time to do what he or she does best
- Follow up on things multiple times until the items are completed

Noise turns into lost productivity, frustration, turnover, health problems, and decreased income.

This book is also for the second-in-command. Most second-in-commands struggle to be successful because they are not aware of what it takes to be effective. I have helped save many second-in-commands' careers with the principles you will read about in this book.

I was actually challenged by a publisher interested in publishing this book who told me I had to define my audience. He didn't like it when I told him, "The first- and second-in–commands." He said it had to be one or the other. I asked him if he had ever read a marriage book that spoke to both the husband and wife. He said he was divorced and had never read any marriage books. That convinced me that I needed to write to both the first-in-command and the second-in-command.

This book will give the first- and second-in-command the principles to make the noise go away for the first-in-command. But it will also make the noise go away just as much for the second-in-command. It might help create a much more successful career for that second-in-command as well.

I met Ken Koller, who has been a great help in writing this book, in 2006 when he became a second-in-command for one of my clients. Ken Koller has also spent most of his career as an effective second-in-command. Ken enhances the concepts in the book through his many experiences as both a first- and second-in-command.

We chose a parable style because I knew that first- and second-in-commands would want a quick read that keeps their attention, one that is memorable because of the stories. The setting is a mountain cabin, where the first- and second-in-command are on a retreat to understand how the noise went away over a three-year period for the first-in-command.

You will read my experiences and many experiences of the first- and second-in-commands I have worked with over the last fifteen years.

I will also give insights as to the hiring qualities of an effective second-in-command and ideas on how to keep a good one when you get one.

The noise will go away when you apply these principles as a first- or second-in-command.

Chapter 1

THE NOISE

J IM SAT ON THE back porch of his new vacation home in the mountains of Colorado, reflecting on how his life had changed over the last three years. It had been three years since Jim had hired Brett Giles as his second-in-command at Golden Electric Supply. As Jim sipped on his coffee on this cool and crisp spring morning, he reflected on the transformation that had occurred in his life.

Jim Clancy had started the company eighteen years earlier at the seasoned age of thirty-five with a great work ethic and substantial debt. He had envisioned a great and exciting life of being a business owner. World travel, plenty of time off, unlimited family time, and more money than he could spend were all within his grasp. He was a business owner!

It wasn't long before reality hit like a punch in the gut from a heavyweight boxer. Owning a business was delivering the opposite of his dream and was primarily responsible for transforming his thick, coal black hair to a crop that was now totally snow white. He was never able to get time off and rarely saw his family. The income was marginal because he was too busy to do what made him the most profit. He didn't have time to do the things that he loved to do. He found himself spending time on the details of his business and dealing with things that constantly frustrated him and drained his energy.

His life was filled with noise—so many things going on in his head. Noise came in many forms. Noise showed up as lack of communication, things falling through the cracks, people not thinking, and others not showing they really cared about the business. He wasn't sleeping, and his mind was always running through all the things going on in the business. He had lost the time and focus to work on things he loved to do and was really good at doing. The noise kept him from reaching his and his company's potential. He felt all alone, and it sure was noisy at the top.

Jim had found out what most business owners eventually come to realize: owning a business can easily turn into the business owning you. He constantly had to explain to his wife and children why he couldn't spend more time with them. It didn't take long before the business had taken over his life and was negatively affecting his family life.

He had seen other entrepreneurs reach financial freedom, travel, and be very involved with their families … and he was frustrated and envious. "Why can't I have that?" he thought. "What are they doing that allows them this freedom?"

He knew that if he could make the noise go away, he could have this freedom.

The noise did go away, and the freedom followed. Now Jim sat on the quiet back porch of his beautiful new mountain home in Colorado. Three years ago Jim had made the most critical strategic decision since beginning his company. He had hired the right second-in-command. That second-in-command was Brett Giles, and Brett had made the noise go away.

Chapter 2

THE POWER OF AN EFFECTIVE SECOND-IN-COMMAND

B RETT GILES WAS A local businessman whom Jim had run across numerous times over his career. Brett seemed intelligent and presented himself very well. He had a reputation of being a strong manager and leader. Jim thought hiring Brett as a second-in-command could solve his "noise" problem. After a few months of discussions, Brett decided to join Jim and become his second-in-command.

Jim had tried other second-in-commands, but this time it worked. Looking back over the past three years, he was amazed at how quickly the noise had gone away.

He reflected as he kicked back early on this Saturday morning in his porch chair, enjoying the peaceful view of his twenty-five acres of blue spruce trees, a sparkling stream, and tall, grassy open meadows. Jim was counting his blessings. He finally had the time to coach his kids' sports teams, had built his beautiful dream home, and was spending a lot of time with his family. He had achieved what he had always dreamed was possible as a business owner ... financial and personal freedom! The transition from being owned by the business to total freedom had seemed to take place overnight. He was now working "on" the business and not "in" the business!

He was enjoying his dream mountain getaway in one of the

3

places where he would be spending quality time with his family and friends.

"What the heck are you staring at?" Brett chirped as he pushed the sliding glass door open and strolled out of the house with a couple of cups of fresh coffee.

Jim looked up at his second-in-command and grinned as Brett handed him a cup. Brett wore his mountain-biking clothes and had already been out on an early morning ride. He was athletic and driven. The 195 pounds that clung to his six-feet-three inch frame were in contrast to Jim's more average height and build. Brett loved to work hard, and he played hard. Mountain biking was his outlet, his relief, to eliminate the stress of the business world.

Jim responded to Brett's question while he continued to look out over the second-story balcony. "I was wondering how I went from working day and night, twenty-four-seven, and never seeing my family, to relaxing at my vacation home and not having to even think about the company."

"Well, isn't that why we came up here?" Brett snapped back, attempting to get the discussion started. Brett enjoyed their verbal bantering, especially in this comfortable, unofficial setting. It was the kind of bantering that unlocked their senses of humor but also reflected their respect for one another. Brett was fifteen years younger than Jim, but their age difference was never a factor in their peer to peer relationship.

Jim and Brett had decided to get away for the specific purpose of analyzing the concept of "second-in-command" to see if they could determine why it was working so well. Jim was concerned that if they didn't understand why it was working it could fall apart in the future. They wanted to capture all the factors that had led to this outcome.

Brett began, "Let's get started on this project so I can get out on that mountain and do some more biking."

The porch deck was very large and faced a steep mountain. The home's two-story design gave way to beautiful views. Brett started moving the chairs to the middle area of the porch deck and set up an easel and flip chart at the corner, next to the huge glass window that reflected the beautiful view of the mountain.

Brett was quick-witted and fun, but he was always the driver of productivity. He had a tendency to be a little pragmatic. He began the conversation. "Let's set an agenda for our weekend. I want to make sure we capture all the things that made the noise go away and what we need to do to keep things that way. Why don't we start with the end in mind? We should define what it looks like when the noise is gone."

Jim liked the way Brett jumped in and took charge of planning sessions like this. Brett was a natural at organizing things. He nodded his head to tell Brett he was on track and to keep rolling.

Brett continued, "The second thing we need to do is brainstorm about what you think made the noise go away. We can capture each item on the flip chart, and then we can work through the details of each one. How does that sound?"

Jim was a typical first-in-command who had a short attention span and was quickly distracted. A structure that showed him where he was heading was helpful and gave him a good feeling about how they were starting. He confirmed Brett's direction with a quick response. "Let's do it!"

Brett walked over to the flip chart and grabbed a marker. "Okay, Jim, you've given me a lot of clarity about how bad things were before I came to Golden Electric. Heck, I experienced a lot of it myself. I know our goal is to understand what made the noise go away for you, but I want to make sure I have clarity on the ultimate outcome. Let's build a list of what it looks or feels like when the noise is gone."

Jim's excitement about this exercise showed immediately as he jumped up and asked for the marker. He wanted to write this list on the flip chart.

Jim began, "My life is so much better with a strong second-in-command. The least I can do is give you a rest and write this stuff down myself." He began writing, speaking about each item as he wrote.

"Number one, I'm doing what I love to do. It reminds me of what I dreamed of when I thought about being a business owner.

"Number two, my focus is like a laser. I don't have to get in the middle of everyone's business because of my wondering, curious mind. My confidence in the organization, and my second-in-command, allows me to keep this laser focus.

"Number three, I'm not worrying nearly as much. People are proactively communicating to me about what is going on in critical areas of the business before I feel the need to check on them.

"Number four, my family is getting to see me a lot more. As a matter of fact, my wife told me I was getting in her business too much. Maybe we need a second-in-command at home?"

Brett responded quickly, "My advice is to keep that thought inside and *never* let it out again. Debi wouldn't appreciate that idea."

Jim saw the wisdom in the comment, and after a good laugh he nodded his head in agreement.

He continued, "Okay, number five. Less stress and hopefully a longer life. I feel younger and more energetic without all that stress from before.

"Let's see … number six would be staff productivity. The organization is doing much better without me looking into every detail and causing chaos. There is no question that my behavior used to cause priority problems and a lot of frustration among the staff. As the owner of the company, when I would address issues with front line employees, it would confuse them as to what is most important. With me staying out of the way, the are much more productive, and I think, or maybe *hope*, that they like me more. This has clearly been a big part of our increased productivity and profitability.

"Number seven, of course, is more profit. This is a very nice benefit of making the noise go away.

"Okay, I can't believe I almost forgot perpetuation. I want to sell this business some day. A friend told me years ago that financial and leadership perpetuation are two different things. The financial perpetuation strategy has been in place, but leadership perpetuation is just now starting to take shape. This is a critical part of our future success. Perpetuation is definitely an important element of the noise being gone."

"Jim, was that number eight?" Brett was following along, and Jim hadn't written down the number. He wasn't sure if Jim wanted perpetuation to be a separate item.

"Yeah, number eight," Jim said as he walked over to the edge of the deck and looked into the distance.

After a minute or two of Jim standing and staring into the

distant mountains, Brett asked, "Are you finished or just having a senior moment?"

"I'm doing both, Mr. Impatient!" Jim quickly responded with a teasing bark.

After a quick laugh, Brett tore off the page and stuck it to the big window. He spoke with authority as he gave direction and purpose to the list, "We need to keep focused on this list as we investigate what made the noise go away, Jim."

Jim agreed with a nod as he went back to sit down in his comfortable chair.

Chapter 3

PRINCIPLES THAT MAKE THE NOISE GO AWAY

B RETT WALKED OVER TO the flip chart and wrote, Principles That Made the Noise Go Away. He turned toward Jim and said, "You're on such a roll. Why don't you tell me what you think made the noise go away. Then we'll be able to get some clarity on what we have to do to make sure these items stay in place in the future."

Jim stared at the pad of paper. He couldn't determine where to start.

Brett saw him struggling and stimulated the conversation. Empathy wasn't a natural gift; he was just using one of his professional tactics. "Okay, so you hired a couple of people to fill the position of second-in-command. It obviously wasn't just having a warm body in the job that changed your life. You had people in the job before me, and it didn't change your thinking or your company. What was it that caused the transformation? Just say what comes to your mind."

This was the trigger Jim needed. He began to unleash the flood of ideas and thoughts that had been scrambled in his brain these past three years. Brett feverishly jotted them down, capturing and organizing Jim's thoughts.

Principles That Made the Noise Go Away

o   Upward communication

o   I'm doing what I enjoy and do best. You kept me informed.

o   Keeping priorities: you helped us establish our priorities, and you have helped us stay on track.

o   You brought new ideas and value to the business.

o   You seemed to be losing sleep for me.

o   You spend time with our customers, which gives me confidence that you understand them.

o   You seem to find unique ways to make our company, and me, look good to others.

o   You lead others to do things versus doing everything yourself.

o   You solve problems very well.

o   You get results.

Brett stood for a moment looking at the list. "WOW," he said jestfully. "Sounds like I need a raise."

"Uh-oh. It sure is getting noisy out here," Jim responded.

"I'm just kidding, Jim. Isn't this supposed to be fun?"

They laughed, but Jim had something on his mind that he felt he had to convey to Brett. Jim was very philosophical and liked to look at the deeper meaning behind why things worked. After looking over the balcony for a few seconds, Jim expressed what was on his mind. "Business is a game of anticipating trends, behaviors, and results. But the game isn't mechanical. It's driven by human behavior that drives economic activity. You can't anticipate what or when people will do different things. So I'm compelled to see what is happening, watch trends, and continually look for what might go wrong. The reason I have to do that is because I don't know if anyone else is doing it, or even cares! When the items we listed on that chart are accomplished, it gives me confidence and frees me from thinking about what might happen in the business that I'm not anticipating. People's behavior creates noise in my head, and when you do this stuff," he said, pointing to the flip chart, "the noise goes away!" Jim was very animated as he finished this thought.

Brett could feel the passion and was inspired by the fact that Jim realized he was part of the solution. "So if these are the items that have made the noise go away, we need to get into each one and understand them."

Jim jumped up and spoke as he was walking inside. "Not before we get another cup of coffee."

"Now you're talking," Brett responded as he followed Jim into the cabin.

Chapter 4

UPWARD COMMUNICATION

FTER THE TWO OF them had coffee and made some small talk about a few issues back at the office, they came back to the porch and prepared to take on the list.

"Jim, I think we just need to take one item at a time and extract the details of what made the noise go away," Brett said.

Jim anxiously jumped in. "The one that stands out to me is Upward Communication. Let's start with that."

Brett nodded. He walked over to the flip chart and grabbed a marker.

Jim sat in one of the comfortable chairs next to the railing and put his feet up on the wood table. He continued, "You standing in front of that flip chart just triggered my memory of when you first made the noise go away for me. It was about six months after you started with the company. I was sitting in my office, as stressed as I've ever been. I hadn't slept very well for the past few days, and my mind was running a hundred miles an hour. I didn't feel like I had control of anything that was going on. You set up a flip chart and asked me to start listing what was keeping me up at night. Hey! I'm seeing a trend here with this flip chart thing! Maybe that's why you're so successful as a second-in-command!"

Brett smirked and shook his head as he tried to not laugh at Jim's feeble attempt at humor. "Okay, funny boy, I don't think we're going to get anywhere if you keep this up."

11

Jim continued with his story. "Okay. You were taking notes on the pad while I expressed what was keeping me up at night. I told you that I was concerned about our line of credit, employee training, and the upcoming inventory assessment. You looked at me and told me not to worry about any of those items. You said you would look into them, make sure we were proactively managing them, and get back to me. I have to tell you that I didn't feel very confident at that point because with you being so new, I didn't know if you had any idea what you were doing.

"What you did over the next few weeks was the beginning of my new life. You took all three issues and not only managed them, but you kept me informed. The actual management of those items didn't seem to be the key to giving me confidence; it was how you communicated that did the job. Every day for the next few weeks you gave me an update on what was happening in all three areas.

"After about three weeks of this I found myself sleeping better again. I guess the key to my feeling confident and trusting you had everything to do with how you communicate with me."

Brett jumped in. "Okay, that sounds good, but I can't believe that I'm a great communicator. My wife sure doesn't think I am. What was it about the communication that made the noise go away for you?"

Jim responded with a sense of clarity. "For most of my career I was labeled as a micromanager. I seemed to be frequently checking into what our employees were doing. They would get mad at me and tell me to let them do their jobs. I just couldn't bring myself to do it. I know I caused chaos and frustration. And I'm sure it was frustrating to them. But I *had* to know what was going on. They just don't understand that it is my butt on the line around here and I don't ever want to lose this place!

"Checking with me on what was keeping me up at night and keeping me informed on how those things were progressing enabled me to focus on other things," Jim added. "I don't need to worry about things when I'm kept of aware of them on a frequent basis!"

Brett wanted to make sure he understood Jim's comments. "Are you talking about the items you delegate to me, or is it more?" he asked.

Jim quickly replied, "No, I believe our delegation process works fine. I'm talking about how you find out what is most important to me and keep me informed of what is going on in those areas!"

Brett smiled because he had been purposeful in his communication strategy with Jim, but he hadn't known it would be the key to his success as an effective second-in-command. He was also smiling because he was realizing what a positive impact he was having on Jim. "I think we may have found our first jewel, Jim."

Jim leaned back in his chair as if to absorb the depth and significance of this issue. He thought about how this process seemed so simple but really took a lot of noise away.

Brett was thinking about how to explain what he was really doing with this process.

After about a minute of silence, Jim was the first to speak. "Yeah, I think we're on to something. Let me try to summarize it in a single statement. You extracted what was important to me, and you gave frequent communication on the activity and progress in those areas. I tell you what—just expressing those thoughts makes the noise go away."

Brett responded with a tinge of arrogance. "This isn't a new invention, Jim, and I actually do more than just ask you what you're thinking about. I'm pretty purposeful in this area of helping you feel confident about what goes on around here. I consistently ask each week what's keeping you up at night, but I also find out what is important through other techniques. I listen and observe you constantly to see what is taking you away from what you do best. If you speak to employees, you'll find out that I listen to what you're talking about."

"You better be listening to me," Jim said with a laugh as he adjusted in his chair.

Brett laughed. "Yes, as hard as it might be at times, I listen and I observe where you spend your time. If you dig into something it can be a sign that you're experiencing noise in that area. I record a list of these items, stay appraised of their status, and then maintain proactive communications with you until they're completed. It takes a lot of work, but I guarantee it would be more work for me if I wasn't staying proactive on these items.

"One of the things I've observed," Brett noted, "is that the list is much shorter now than it was three years ago. I'm confident that your being informed of what is going on in areas that keep you up at night keeps the noise away from you and helps you stay focused on what you do best.

"And I believe you trust me more because you have confidence in a few areas I manage. This is because you know from our history that I'm always on top of those issues. I don't think that would've happened if I just did those things without communicating the status. The success has come because the proactive communication kept you informed on those items until you felt confident they were going to get accomplished. I still make sure to keep you informed in a few of those areas every few weeks or months because I anticipate your instinctive nature and obsessive need to know."

Jim thought about Brett's last statement for a moment and responded, "I would have to agree. What excites me is that keeping me informed allows me to spend a lot more time doing what I do best, and that makes us a lot of money. I can't believe how simple this concept is but hard to get someone to execute. I know a lot of second-in-commands who wouldn't want to do this process. They would say the first-in-command needs to trust them and let them do their job. They would say it is the first-in-command's responsibility to trust the organization to do what needs to be done. Those second-in-commands don't understand the mind of a first-in-command. We are compelled to look into what is keeping us up at night. Your process is simple yet brilliant. Brett, do you have a formal process you're already using, or is it just up there rolling around in your head?"

Brett proudly admitted, "Yes, I have a process, and it looks like it's worth continuing. I developed a form that I use, and it seems to work really well."

"Okay, let's see the form and make it a part of our weekend work product."

Brett fumbled through his briefcase. "It's right here. The form works well for me now, but I'm willing to modify it if we need to."

	UP AT NIGHT LIST			
ITEM	DESIRED RESULT	ACTIVITY	STATUS	TARGET DATE

Jim looked the form over. "This is great, Brett! I think we're on our way to truly uncovering what makes you an effective second-in-command."

Brett's compulsion to be organized kicked in at this point. "We have to record all of our ideas and insights from this weekend. It will help us to remember and build on what we're doing, and heck, maybe I'll write a book someday. For each item we work with, I think we should identify action items for the first-in-command and action items for the second-in-command. I will call these takeaways." He wrote Proactive Communication and then First-in-Command Takeaways and Second-in-Command Takeaways.

He explained to Jim, "I think this is a good way to capture what we've been doing." He recorded the takeaway actions for the first- and second-in-command.

UPWARD COMMUNICATION

First-in-Command Duties

o   Identify and communicate what is keeping him or her up at night.

o   Look at weekly updates to stay informed.

Second-in-Command Duties

o   Ask what is keeping the first-in-command up at night.

o   Observe what the first-in-command is focusing on and where he or she spends his time.

o   Proactively communicate updates and changes in areas keeping the first-in-command up at night.

o   Make sure to communicate in the form most effective for the first-in-command.

Jim had walked over to the other end of the porch. He was leaning over the edge, watching a deer go around the side of the house, when Brett spoke to reengage him. "Jim, how often do you want to get this proactive communication?"

"What's wrong with what we've been doing?" Jim said without any thought.

Brett shrugged his shoulders and leaned against the frame of the big windows, as if to say it didn't need to change.

Jim thought about the question for a minute and said, "If you and I continued to meet every Friday, I could be more prepared to tell you what's keeping me up at night, and then I would get to have a relaxing weekend." The relief on his face was visible as he spoke. With another attempt at humor, he quipped, "Hey, now I know why I pay you so much! You get to take that stuff home with you over the weekend and not me!"

Brett quickly responded with a laugh. "Thanks a lot ... did I mention I need a raise?"

"Okay, back to the communication process," Jim said quickly, as if to jokingly defuse the raise issue. "So we keep meeting on Fridays, and then you communicate with me on each item as it is logical. Some items will require weekly communication, but others will require daily or possibly monthly updates. Let's develop a new form to keep up with those items separately."

"Whoa! Wait a minute," Brett responded. "This process is in place and working very well. If you look at the right side of the form, you'll see I have a column for how often you need updates and communication. The only thing we need to add to the process is your knowledge that it's happening. You'll be able to bring more value to the process because you'll be prepared and purposeful in helping me know what's keeping you up at night. This will bring great value because it will eliminate some of the guesswork."

Jim agreed. He felt confident with what Brett had said. He was already happy with Brett, and he could see how bringing the specific items to light was going to make him better at helping Brett make even more noise go away.

Jim spoke with excitement. "Great! I'll make sure to tell you what's keeping me up at night, and then I'll tell you how often I need updates and communication on each item. I think we have it. Making the noise go away really does seem to have a lot to do with your proactive communication. I can't wait to dig into these other concepts. Where should we go from here?"

In his normal confident tone, Brett suggested, "Let's go back to our list of what makes the noise go away for you. Let's check off Upward Communication. Now we have to choose which item we want to take on next."

Jim stood up and walked to the door. "I don't know about you, but all this work has made me hungry. Let's go make some sandwiches while we keep working."

Brett tossed the marker on the table next to the flip chart. "You don't have to tell me twice."

Chapter 5

A PROBLEM SOLVER

THE MORNING'S ENERGETIC DIALOGUE had triggered quite an appetite in the two of them. In the kitchen they could still see the mountain landscape out of the beautiful, tall windows. They made a couple of large sandwiches and got out chips and fruit to fuel the energy they needed for the afternoon session. They sat at the kitchen table to eat and change the environment a little. As they placed the food on the table, Brett suggested a strategy for the afternoon.

"Why don't we take a look at the list of items that made the noise go away and go as hard as we can until dinner?"

Jim liked the idea and walked onto the back porch to look at the list and see which one he wanted to start with.

Jim walked back into the kitchen with a big smile on his face. "I have the right one for us to go over during lunch. It's one I know made the noise go away for me, and it's one that you will do most of the talking about. That way I can focus my attention on eating."

Brett responded with a mumble and a grunt as he quickly bit into his sandwich. He expected Jim to be strategic about everything. Why wouldn't he be strategic to his advantage during lunch as well?

"Okay, what do you need me to pontificate about now?" Brett choked out with his last bite.

"Before you became my second-in-command I was a crap

magnet. Seems like everyone in the organization brought their problems to me. I couldn't seem to find anyone who made good decisions on their own. One difference between you and all the other second-in-commands, and anyone else in our company for that matter, is your ability to make good decisions when you're solving problems. You seem to have made an impact on the entire organizations ability to make decisions. Don't get me wrong—you're a smart guy, but you can't be that smart, and you certainly can't be the only person solving problems."

Brett rolled his eyes in response while Jim continued. "I have all the confidence in the world with you solving a problem in my company. I have never had that confidence or felt that safe with others in the past. When you take something on I know we'll have an acceptable and well-thought-out solution. So while I eat, give me insights as to what makes you a good problem solver."

"Okay, Jim, I think I know what you're talking about. By the way, thanks for the confidence in my intelligence. I guess we don't have to worry about adding intelligence to the list of attributes of a second-in-command who makes the noise go away. Before I tell you my secret, what the heck is a crap magnet?"

Brett could tell it was a painful term for Jim as he closed his eyes, leaned forward, put his face down in his hands, and began to explain. "Let me tell you about a day about a month before you came on board. On this particular morning, I was excited about the day, and my energy level was very high when I arrived. As usual, I had plenty to do, and I looked forward to getting to my office to knock out a productive day.

"My day was planned well, since I'd been spinning ideas around in my head most of the weekend. I was all smiles as I walked in the front door and saw Linda, who used to be our receptionist. I said hello with a cheerful voice of confidence and excitement. She responded just as welcomingly and grabbed a stack of notes and mail for me. 'Mr. Clancy, I have a few messages here for you,' she said. I responded positively, as my day was still filled with hope. The first few messages were simply phone calls to return. The next two messages were personnel needing something from me. 'They both asked if I would let you know they need to see you,' she said.

"I reacted positively, but something told me that my day was about to change, and I could feel a little energy begin to leave my body. I was hoping to get right on my planned projects, but I told myself that a few moments spent returning calls and meeting with my managers should be okay. It wouldn't kill the day, I hoped, still retaining some level of optimism. I departed from the receptionist desk and faced the gauntlet—toward my office.

"The stack of messages from Linda and the need to see a couple of managers was starting to ruin my optimism. I really wasn't looking forward to having to go by everyone to get to my office. I was really starting to wonder why I'd not moved it up closer to the front door years before. But I like to say hello to folks. I don't want to be one of those faceless owners. Still, I was a little leary that day. Any more unanticipated work handed to me could destroy my hope of a productive week.

"I purposely lowered my head and walked toward my office, trying to appear invisible, but with little hope for success. 'Mr. Clancy?' a young sales executive blurted out. I acknowledged her. She proceeded to let me know that she could really use some help with a relationship on one of her accounts. I agreed and wrote it down on my calendar. I took a couple more steps, and my former account manager called from behind me. She asked if I had a few minutes to discuss one of her accounts because she was having problems with it and needed some help. Once again, I agreed. My energy, like a tire with a slow leak, was now getting lower and lower, and my day had just begun.

"I was now halfway across the office. My old second-in-command stepped into the hallway and asked if he could run something by me. 'Of course,' I said. He went through a problem he was dealing with and asked for my advice. We discussed it for a while, and we both took action items away from the twenty-minute discussion. I was now feeling like I was already behind for the day, and it was just eight thirty IN THE MORNING.

"I got closer to my office when Steve, our controller, stopped me and announced, 'We have a problem.' I reluctantly invited him into my office, and we discussed a billing problem that was going to have a negative impact on that month's financial statement. The meeting lasted about forty-five minutes, and again, more action items were built, and I hadn't dealt with a single one of my plans of the day.

"Then, worst of all, one of the telemarketing managers came to my office and informed me of a problem with their script. I saw his face change from hopeful to depressed when he turned the corner to my office. It was like he needed to sell me on taking his problem. He explained why the script wasn't working and asked if I would fix it. Of course I said yes, and he immediately got up to leave the office. You should have seen him. He had the most pitiful look on his face. He seemed so pained that he had this huge problem and it burdened him to have to give it to me. But unknown to him, I followed him out of the office. As he turned the corner and left, he regained a brilliant bounce in his step and displayed a huge smile. His problems, the ones I pay him to solve, had just become mine!

"I know what you're thinking: it's my fault! I allowed this to happen. Brett, I walked through the office and all the crap stuck to me. This is what's known as a crap magnet. I was a crap magnet. This hasn't happen to me since you arrived, and you don't seem to have this problem. So what the heck did you do?"

Brett knew he had to respond just to help Jim breathe again. This was obviously a big issue for him. "A few years ago I went to a seminar on leadership and management. The instructor kept saying that great leaders teach their employees to bring them solutions and not just their problems. Half the day was spent on this concept and methods to get employees to embrace this strategy. I couldn't buy into it. It just didn't seem logical that people would just transform themselves to start creating solutions that didn't exist before they were told to do so. What was going to change?

"I battled with this concept as I tried to implement it with the staff members. One day I was sitting in the office after a really bad day of too many of our people making really bad decisions. They brought solutions, all right; unfortunately they were all terrible solutions. It was evident to me that just bringing solutions was not the answer.

"Now, don't get me wrong, the solutions message was deeper than just bringing a solution. They taught us to give people the proper training and resources to come up with good solutions, but it still just didn't seem to be the right focus. So, that evening, as I thought through what was wrong, I finally realized the true problem."

Jim jumped in and said, "See, you're a natural at problem solving."

Brett was not amused, as he was passionate and excited about his message. "The point of the focus needed to be changed. Employees were focusing on bringing *a* solution to the problem. If a solution was the only goal, all they had to do was come up with any solution and they had met the objective. I knew exactly what had to be done next. We had to go deeper than one solution and get into the consequences of alternative solutions. I called this 'consequence decision making.' I built a consequence worksheet and started using it when I made any decisions. It's very powerful."

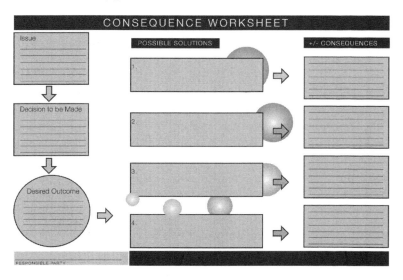

"The worksheet starts by asking you to state the problem. Then you state the desired outcome. The next step is to brainstorm multiple solutions. The sheet then drives you toward evaluating all the positive and negative consequences of each solution. When you understand the possible consequences of a decision, you're able to choose which one has the best possible outcome and which solutions have potential consequences you wouldn't want to live with.

"After using the tool for a few weeks, I introduced it to our employees. They had to come to me for help the first two or three times they had to make a decision. That was okay because they needed the training. However, they stopped coming to me after a while because they started looking deeper into problems and the potential solutions and all the possible consequences. What is really exciting is how conversations I have with them now are more focused on possible consequences of decisions versus problems or solutions. It's a much more stimulating, productive, and fun conversation. They look to me to evaluate consequences rather than to be the person who solves all their problems."

Jim remembered how Brett frequently used the term *consequences* when they discussed possible problems and solutions. He blurted out excitedly, "You've been utilizing my experience to understand potential consequences in decisions you are making, haven't you?"

"I hate to give away all my secrets, but yes, that's exactly what I'm doing. What I have found is that decisions are made more quickly and are usually better decisions. They're more calculated because the consequences are analyzed and the risk-reward analysis is clear. I use this tool when making key decisions, and I lean on your experience to understand the possible consequences. It saves you time and allows me to make good, well-informed decisions. However, I couldn't have made these decisions without your giving me a chance to make them. I was very impressed when I came to Golden Electric Supply that you gave me the freedom to make decisions."

Jim responded with passion, "Don't think it was without watching those decisions closely. I let you make some decisions, but I looked over your shoulder pretty close in the beginning. It wasn't until after I saw a few great solutions to problems that I allowed you this freedom. I don't think I could go very long without checking on the decisions being made once in a while. But the length of time between checking grew longer and longer as you proved yourself."

"Okay," Brett responded. "So it sounds like we both have a role in making me a good problem solver, which makes the noise go away for you. The first-in-command has to give the second-in-command freedom to make decisions but needs to watch closely in the beginning and begin to back away after success is demonstrated. The second-in-command needs to think of and analyze consequences when making decisions. He also needs to teach others in the organization about thinking of consequences and not stopping at the first solution that comes up."

"Write those on the board, Brett. We need to make sure to capture these thoughts."

Brett walked over to the board and started writing. "Okay, let's start with what you as the first-in-command need to do."

A Problem Solver

First-in-Command Duties

o Give the second-in-command freedom to make decisions, but oversee effectiveness of the decisions

o Don't solve problems for others

Second-in-Command Duties

o The second-in-command needs to thoroughly assess the consequences of his/her decisions

o The second-in-command should be willing to mentor subordinates on "consequence decision making"

o Encourage employees to consider alternative solutions and their positive as well as negative consequences before bringing the issue to their supervisor

"Well, Jim, do these items summarize our thoughts accurately?"

"Yeah, and all this thinking has made me awfully thirsty. What do you say we grab some cool lemonade and rest our brains for a spell?"

"Couldn't agree with you more. And I think my marker is drying up!"

Chapter 6

DOING WHAT I ENJOY AND WHAT I DO BEST

J IM AND BRETT FINISHED a couple glasses of lemonade while discussing more examples of how some people struggled at understanding and implementing the consequence model of solving problems. The session gave Jim a great new understanding and appreciation of what a powerful tool the consequence worksheet was and what a fortunate guy he was to have a second-in-command like Brett.

They decided to work on the next topic while getting some exercise. They took off into the mountains on a beautiful trail. Exercise and new scenery would keep the energy going and stimulate their thoughts. A nice breeze had picked up, and it added to the quiet feeling of being in the mountains. The wind pushed through the trees, but it was still calmingly quiet.

They started the walk without saying anything at all. They were enjoying the peacefulness and beauty. Jim thought that there couldn't be too many places better for clear thinking and relaxation. He certainly couldn't think of a place he would rather be even though he was wishing for more oxygen at this high altitude.

"Can you believe this life we've created here, Brett?"

Brett was thinking about the flip chart and all the items left on it. He wondered what item they should tackle next. He kicked his mind into a new gear to answer Jim.

"Yeah, I know what you mean. I wonder what all the first-in-commands without a strong second-in-command are doing back in the business jungle right now."

Jim looked back at Brett and rolled his eyes. "I bet none of the first-in-commands are being pushed up a mountain about to pass out of oxygen deprivation."

"Hey, don't roll your eyes at me. You look ten years younger than you did three years ago, and you seem to be handling this pace pretty well," Brett popped back in jest.

The comment made Jim laugh as he hadn't thought Brett had seen him roll his eyes. He responded, "Okay, okay, I hear you. Let's get back to the list before we get too old to finish it."

Brett asked Jim which item he wanted to discuss since he couldn't remember all the items.

"Why don't we take on Doing What I Enjoy and What I Do Best? That seems to fit the discussion and the hike."

Jim had been thinking about this topic prior to the trip. He and Brett had both attended a program called Strategic Coach®[1] in Toronto, Canada. The program had helped them understand certain abilities and talents that helped them be successful and bring value to others around them.

"Remember when we did the Strategic Coach® Unique Ability® process?" Jim asked. "It was very clear that I bring the most value to those around me and our business when I'm working with suppliers, financial institutions, and clients. Brett, didn't you determine that teaching, coaching, strategic planning, and marketing were your unique talents? I thought it was insightful to get this clarity of strengths, but we initially struggled at allocating the majority of our time to doing those things. We have evolved since that time and are both doing what we do best.

"Do you remember how rigid we were with our management responsibilities when you first started at the company? We had our traditional CEO and VP responsibilities and job titles, but we

---

1   Strategic Coach® offers successful entrepreneurs a unique process for extraordinary growth, higher income, and exceptional quality of life. www.strategiccoach.com

always seemed to get heavily drawn into things that didn't fall into the categories of what we did best. I remember going to lunch with a friend a couple of years ago who seemed to spend the majority of his time doing what he did best. He had a process that worked well for him, and that's when I changed our structure at Golden.

"My friend had been meeting with his management team every Monday morning at six AM. They lined out the priorities for the week. They moved duties around, forgetting job responsibilities and focusing on unique abilities and talents. The clarity it gave them, and the focus on what they did best, was very attractive and ultimately very successful. I know we didn't formally put this in place at Golden, but I started having Monday morning meetings with you because of my discussions with my friend. I think this is a big reason for our doing what we do best. Our weekly meeting to shuffle our duties based on what we do best and utilize the best use of time makes work a lot more fun."

This monologue triggered an idea for Brett. "We don't just distribute duties between us. I never thought about it, but every one of those meetings results in tasks that I take away and hand off to others. These are things we would have done ourselves in the past, but these meetings make us focus so much on what we do best and the importance of being more productive and getting a better return on investment. We've become an organization based on the highest and best use of our combined talents. You and I are doing what we do best and what brings the highest value to the organization. The return on our time has been incredible," Brett concluded.

Brett's excitement gave Jim energy, and he picked up his pace up the mountain. Brett, also energized, kept in step.

Brett kicked the conversation back in gear. "I can remember weeks when I didn't perform one single item of my unique talents list prior to these meetings. Now, eighty percent of my week is focused on doing what I do best."

Making sure not to lose the momentum of the moment, Jim added, "So what do we do to make this continue to work and possibly improve on it?"

"The Monday meeting seems to be working. This is the most valuable hour we have each week. The accountability to stay focused on what we do best is critical. Now that we've named and defined that time better, I would say we can improve on what we were doing by using 'highest and best use of talent' as our litmus test to determine who takes on what assignments each week."

"I also think we have to be diligent to make sure we delegate items to others if we have priorities that are not in our highest and best use wheelhouse."

"Another thing I would suggest is to make sure we have those meetings, Jim. You've missed quite a few of them because of travel or other interruptions. If we can't meet on a Monday, we need to move it back to Friday and tie it into our communication meeting so it happens. The important thing is that we meet whatever day we decide," Brett emphasized. "The meeting provides a great return on investment, and it absolutely must happen."

Jim stopped for moment, thinking and trying to catch his breath. He agreed with Brett on the topic, but his mind wandered toward the future. "What about when our company grows larger? How will this process work for us then?"

"I think the process will still have great value. If we're going to continue to make the noise go away for you, we need to have this kind of frequent, dedicated conversation. It may have to be a very focused and purposeful meeting with more people involved. But I can't think of a better way to keep a first-in-command focused on what will bring the greatest value to the company. It may need to go to every two weeks eventually, but we can make that decision when the time comes."

Jim agreed with a strong and reassuring nod of the head.

They arrived back at the cabin a few minutes later, and Brett went back to the flip chart to record the takeaways.

Doing What I Enjoy and What I Do Best

First-in-Command Duties

o *Identify unique abilities and natural talents*

o *Share these abilities and talents with the second-in-command*

- o   Monitor my activities to make sure I am staying inside of these abilities and talents the majority of the time

- o   Trade off duties with the second-in-command to establish highest and best use of talent

Second-in-Command Duties

- o   Identify unique abilities and natural talents

- o   Share these abilities and talents with the first-in-command

- o   Monitor yours and the first-in-command's activities to make sure you are both staying inside of these talents the majority of the time

- o   Manage the trade-off of duties

Chapter 7

KEEPING PRIORITIES

"**O**KAY, BRETT, YOU LOOK like you have something on your mind. What are you thinking?"

Jim was correct. Brett was staring at the flip chart trying to put his thoughts together. "This Keeping Priorities item is a big one to me. I remember a few times in the past couple of years when you gave me that 'I feel safe' look, and the noise seemed to have really gone away."

"The 'I feel safe' look? What the heck is that?" Jim responded defensively.

"The same look you've had the last couple days when we hit on the core of any of these issues. It's like you go into this relaxed posture where the weight of the world has just dropped off your shoulders. You break into a big smile—or should I say smirk?" Brett was almost scolding Jim as a reminder of how well this was working for him.

"Okay, I get it," Jim said flippantly. "So enlighten me with another one of those moments."

"How about right after the first year I'd been at Golden? It was January, and you had just returned from another one of those classes where you got a ton of new ideas. You know, the electrical contractors conference; everyone in the company used to be terrified knowing you were there. They just knew you would come back with tons of ideas we would never be able to implement."

Jim didn't seem amused, but he knew exactly what Brett was talking about.

Brett continued. "So you called me into your office, where you had compiled what appeared to be a tower of paper. You informed me that we were going to sort through the two-foot stack of ideas to choose which ones I would implement. That's when I had an idea. I distracted you—told you to go get your organizer—so we could start. While you were gone, I took three pieces of paper and wrote one word in large print on each of them: 'now,' 'no,' and 'later.' They were side by side on the table when you came back. I informed you that we would go through your stack of great ideas and place them in three piles according to the three different priorities.

"The criteria used to determine which pile the idea went into was based on the following: if the item met our immediate needs, followed our strategic direction, and would give us an acceptable return on investment, we would place it in the 'now' file. I would be responsible for making sure the items in this pile were immediately moved forward into action items.

If the item was a great idea but should be executed at a later date, we placed it in the 'later' file. I would place those items in a file to review at our annual strategic planning session.

"If the item did not meet our needs, was outside of our company direction, or would not give us an acceptable ROI, it would go in the 'no' file. That file would be placed in the trash before we left the conference room.

"Of course, you had to lighten up things and be cute, even though you knew the idea was a brilliant way to get things off your plate and out of that cabinet behind your desk. You directed me to retrieve some markers from the other room—nice distraction, by the way—so we could write on the papers. When I returned, you had placed all three pages upside down in one pile and had written, 'Yes, sir! Right away, sir!' on the top page. Then you said, 'This is how I would like to proceed with the project.' Any of this ring a bell?"

Jim was laughing out loud at this point. "I had forgotten all about that little incident. I'm a pretty funny guy, aren't I?"

"Yes, just hilarious," Brett responded sarcastically. "But despite your being so funny, we uncovered why most of your ideas never got off the ground. You lacked follow through and follow-up. You thought that if you had ideas and shared them with others in the organization, then those ideas would somehow get executed. The reality was that you had great ideas and communicated them, and nothing happened. More importantly, you thought they were being implemented, but they weren't.

"The other issue I saw when I first came here was the randomness of what was implemented. We took on ideas as they came to us versus being purposeful and consistent with our strategic plan. When we developed a clear vision and were strategic about how we would get there, we were able to filter new ideas against these plans."

Jim leaped out of his chair with disgust. "All right, here we go again. For the last twenty years of my life people have insinuated I was a poor manager and even bluntly told me I was a bad person for suggesting so many ideas. I'm tired of it! This business wouldn't be as successful as it is without my ideas. I go to seminars, participate in industry groups, read incessantly, and constantly think about ways to improve our operations so we can not only stay in business, but thrive. I have to bring ideas back, and I don't think I'm an evil person for doing it."

"Can I get you lemonade or a beer, Jim?" Jim shook his head to indicate he did not want anything. Brett thought maybe a calming moment was needed. He had observed Jim's natural instinct for innovation and creativity. He knew it was a great value and needed to be cultivated. "Jim, I know it's not only a good thing for our business to benefit from your ideas; it's necessary. We need a visionary and someone bringing innovation to keep us ahead of our competition. You do this as well as anyone I know. However, as a second-in-command my job is to keep us focused on our priorities. We can't run a race going side to side down the street.

"A buddy of mine in Idaho used to tell me about his faithful trail dog, Boomer. When my friend rode his horse in the Rockies he took Boomer along. Boomer was just full of energy. On a typical trail ride my friend would cover twenty miles in a day, and Boomer would travel at least forty miles during the same ride. Boomer would run up and down the trail chasing who knows what while my buddy's horse plodded along the trail focused on getting from point A to point B, just like he planned. My point is, do we want to follow Boomer's lead and inefficiently chase one idea after another? Or do we want to stay on the trail that our strategic plan has laid out for us, remaining focused on those priorities that will provide the best ROI and get us to where we want to go in the most efficient manner?"

Jim chuckled to himself. Then he said with a smile, "So now I have a choice of being a trail dog or a horse!"

Brett responded, "If the horseshoe fits, wear it! Seriously, the analogy is appropriate. We have to have a clear path and be committed to following it.

"You know, Jim, a couple of years ago I realized this incredible talent you have. I felt the need to keep you energized to bring new ideas but make sure we maintained focus and maintained our strategic approach. Here's how I manage this process. First, I encourage you and frequently ask you about ideas and innovative strategies. I don't want you to feel guilty about using your natural instincts. Second, I take those ideas and capture them on a master idea list. You know the one I'm talking about. It's in the back of my planner. I pull it out every time you get creative or give feedback from an event you go to."

Jim connected with his words. He recalled frequent times when Brett had pulled out the back pages of the planner. "I know what you're talking about. That does make me feel safe. When you write those things down I feel like I can let them go. I used to have to store those ideas in my head, in piles on my desk, and in that cabinet behind my desk. It feels good to know that someone feels ownership in these ideas besides me."

Brett liked hearing that this made Jim feel safe, even though he had always assumed so. "After I put the ideas in the planner, I use the 'now,' 'no,' 'later' concept. The 'now' items get put into action and are communicated to the organization regarding how they fit in our strategic plan. The 'later' items go into the quarterly plan review file so we can discuss them at our executive team meetings. We will continue to do this because many of those items are great ideas; they just have to be implemented at the right time. The 'no' items go away. These ideas either won't give us a good return on investment or won't fit with our strategic objectives. My responsibility is to facilitate this discussion and help you decide where each item will end up. But I have to have the freedom to challenge you and give my input as to where I think each item should go."

This strategy was working for Jim, and it truly made the noise go away. It made him realize that he could be his natural self and come up with all the ideas he wanted. "Brett, we need to get the takeaway items for the two of us. I think my job is to keep thinking of great ideas and then trust you to prioritize them and get them in the right action category."

"That's right, Jim, and my job is to make sure to categorize the ideas and put them into action when the time is right. It's also my job to keep you informed of when those items are executed and give you progress reports as they are implemented. This goes back to the proactive communication strategy. It seems like you have more confidence and work toward even greater ideas when you see results from past ideas."

"You're right there, Brett. I do get more energy when we see positive results."

"Speaking of energy, I have none left. I'm starving."

Keeping Priorities

First-in-Command Duties

o   Think of new ideas.

o   Pass off the new ideas to the second-in-command.

o   Allow the process of categorization to work.

o   Remember that not all ideas are good ideas.

Second-in-Command Duties

o   Categorize new ideas in Now, No, Later files

- o *Spend the time to make sure the Now items fit the strategic plan and are developed and implemented.*

- o *Build a file for the Later items to give confidence to the first-in-command that the items will be brought up at the right time.*

- o *Kill the No ideas but be sensitive to the first-in-command's "ownership" of those ideas.*

- o *Encourage the first-in-command to bring new ideas.*

Brett looked at his watch. He couldn't believe it was time for dinner. "This afternoon has gone fast. Let's get cleaned up and go to that nice steak house in town."

"I think I'll put that in the NOW column." Jim headed toward the bedroom to clean up.

Brett just stood there smiling in response to Jim's crative humor. He loved working for Jim, and quick remarks like that were part of the reason why.

Chapter 8

ALIGNING WITH OWNER VALUES

T HE RESTAURANT WAS A great place to relax and continue the discussion. After they ordered their food Jim began to tell Brett about a recent experience at home.

"I had an interesting thing happen at home the other day. One of my daughters, Tiffany, was selected for a traveling soccer team a few months ago. We made a decision as a family to commit to this team. Last week we were presented with the Thanksgiving tournament options in Arizona. I approached my wife that evening to ask her if we all wanted to go or if just one parent or no parent should go with her. One option was left off the list. My wife responded, 'None of us, including our daughter, is going to that tournament.' I immediately reacted—not very bright of me—and said, 'No, our daughter is going to go.'

"I had thought the question was who was going to go, not whether someone was going. She went on to tell me that in her family Thanksgiving was an important holiday, a day when all the family would get together. Soccer was not the most important thing, and they would have to play without her. I won't bore you with all the fun details of the remainder of that discussion, but I will tell you that I won the argument."

Brett had to jump on this statement. "You just think you won. Someday you'll tell me the rest of that story!"

"Normally I would agree with you, Brett. But this time I was able to convince her that we had to send our daughter to the tournament. The way I did it was to change the conversation to values. You can probably guess from this conversation what my wife's number one value would be."

"Family," Brett said without hesitation.

"How very perceptive of you. Yes, her number one value is family, and my number one value is integrity, or doing what I say I will do. We discussed this point and realized we didn't have a right or wrong decision to make; we had a value discussion and a decision to make for our family. We ended up chosing integriy over family.

"I learned a lot that day. The first thing I learned was that values are not good or bad. My wife and I spent a few days after this situation looking at our personal values so we could agree on our family values. We looked at a few lists of possible values from the Internet—things like honesty, trust, integrity, family, and a lot more. It became clear to me that these values are not good or bad. They are all good things. When you look at any of those items and try to decide which one would win in a conflict, you quickly see how hard it can be to decide. We narrowed our values down to our family values and agreed on what we were willing to accept as our decision-making guide. It wasn't easy, but it is already making our lives better because we know what to expect and conflict will be avoided.

"The second thing I learned was that what makes a decision bad is if it doesn't align with the desired values of the organization, or in this case, the desired values of the family. Based on our values, my wife and I were both very passionate about what we thought we should do about the tournament. Each of us was convinced the decision would be bad if it didn't go our way. Until we came up with our shared values, we would have continued to see the other person's decisions as bad when this type of conflict came up.

Jim poured a glass of wine for each of them and continued. "The third thing I learned was that I was very lucky to get a second-in-command whose values align with mine."

Brett was confused by this comment. How did this conversation about Jim's daughter turn into being about him?

Jim saw the confusion on Brett's face, so he decided to explain what he meant. "This scenario showed me that decisions have to line up with values or someone is going to get upset. Since I own this company and am responsible for its success, my values will be at the core. Look at Southwest Airlines and Disney. They have established values for their companies. Those values were established by the values and beliefs of the owner. The employees follow the values of the companies, and it is one of the core reasons they are successful. I can't imagine an employee of one of these companies deciding to do things differently because he or she has a different set of values. The employees of those companies decide when they are hired whether they will align with the values of the company. We have never communicated my values to our employees. I guess I can understand why I frequently get upset with employees when they make decisions that don't line up with those values. It isn't fair to our people that they haven't been given this clarity.

"The second-in-command position is so important in the leadership of the company that it's critical for you to have clarity on my values and to be able to accept and make decisions in alignment with those values. That doesn't mean we have the same values. It means the second-in-command must be able to make decisions based on alignment with the first-in-command's values and be okay with it."

"Wow, Jim! This sounds almost dictatorial! Are you saying the values of the employees in our company don't matter?"

"No, of course their values matter. Part of what we do when we hire someone is to see if he or she has values that line up with our company thinking. However, just like my situation at home, if I just went off of my values and didn't discuss it with my wife, I would have been in constant trouble. But since we discussed it, we decided to define and agree on our family values. Now each of us can make decisions for ourselves as they affect us individually, but when it has an effect on the family we use the family values.

"This is exactly what I would expect to happen in my company. Each individual will live up to his or her own values, but when it has an impact on our employees, vendors, clients, or our company, he or she needs to make sure his or her decisions are in alignment with our company values. Because we're a privately held company, those values are mine. If we were a publicly held company or partnership, the values could be determined corporately. I simply need to communicate my values to the people more effectively. The food arrived and they began to eat. They enjoyed the food but both men were deep in thought with every bite. Jim was the first to pause his eating.

"The reason I bring this up, Brett, is that it is actually one of the things you've done to make the noise go away for me. We need to put it on the list of items because I forgot it when I was going through the list the first day. You asked me early in our relationship about my values. I told you the top five, and you've always made sure to make decisions and align yourself with them."

Brett interrupted, "That's interesting, Jim, because I remember doing it but for a different reason. I thought you and I had a lot in common, and I asked because I thought our values were pretty closely matched. Oh, and if you remember, they did. So do you think an effective second-in-command has to have the same values?"

"No way! It would be impossible to find a second-in-command whose values match mine exactly. I don't think husbands and wives have to have the same values either. But I think a marriage relationship requires the determination of joint values, and I think a second-in-command has to be able to accept and run the business based on the values of the company. You were lucky because you already had the values, but others could do the same thing. And if you really think about it, there's sort of a marriage that exists between the first-in-command and the second-in-command. Platonic as it is, it's still a close relationship. Spending eight-to-ten-hour days together makes it close by definition!"

Jim continued. "I was talking to my neighbor, Dan Beaty, from Beaty Construction, and he told me his story the other day before I came up here to the cabin. He had a consultant come in to do some work with his executive team. The team was having some problems because they wanted to do things in the company and Dan was always jumping in, changing decisions and getting frustrated with the way they ran things. The consultant immediately realized that they didn't have clarity on the company's values.

"The consultant did an interesting exercise. He gave the management team a list of about a hundred values. They were given the objective to go around the table, one person at a time, and take one item off the list based on the following criteria: if they had to make a decision, and these items came into conflict, which would lose? For my daughter's soccer tournament, the example would be that family lost out to integrity. The next rule was that if someone disagreed about the item coming off the list, the group would vote. If the majority voted to keep an item on the list the person had to choose a different value.

"This process continued until they reached the final ten items and could defend their list to the consultant. At that point they had to number them backward from ten to one, using the same criteria; each word was challenged by another. He said it was fun to watch them make up examples of how the two different values might come into conflict and see how they would make their decisions based on those values. He also said this painted a very clear picture of how decisions are made in business every day. I digress.

"The next exercise the consultant did was to ask Dan to do the same exercise on his own. The consultant facilitated this discussion and watched him battle with each word along the way. He came down to his final top ten. The consultant then brought Dan and the staff into the same room and asked them to write the two different lists up on the board. The ten items on each list sat side by side, and they, of course, were different. He asked the group to think for a few moments about what having two different lists meant to the organization. They gave many different answers, like: 'We're obviously not on the same page!' and 'We should blend them together to come to a collaborative solution.' Ultimately, they reluctantly suggested that they should start all over; others said the owner needed to accept their list.

"The consultant let them talk for a while, and then he gave them the correct answer. The staff gasped as the consultant erased their list from the board. He told them: 'The reality is that the business owner's list is the only one that really matters.' I can understand this as a first-in-command and business owner. The values of the first-in-command are the values the company has to follow, or the first-in-command will not feel safe and will ultimately be frustrated. The consultant helped them understand this thinking by reminding them that the values listed were all good things. They were honor, integrity, honesty, and items everyone in the group appreciated and agreed with. They just didn't put them as top values for themselves as a group. When they looked at the owner's values again, they all agreed they could make decisions based on those values and the company would be a great place to work.

"You know how we've noticed a lot of second-in-commands who haven't made it in our friends' businesses? I think this is one of the biggest reasons they fail. They don't understand the values of the first-in-command, and they make decisions out of alignment with them. Anyone who consistently makes decisions out of alignment with the first-in-command's values will not be in an organization very long."

Brett was finally connecting with the concept and understood what Jim was saying. "So it seems critical that a first-in-command has to communicate his or her values to the organization. Let me get a piece of paper from our server and write this down. It has to go on our flip chart when we get back. So it is incumbent on the first-in-command to clearly and consistently communicate his or her values through the entire organization. If a second-in-command has been identified then it's imperative that the first-in-command and the second-in-command are in lockstep as to what values are desired for the business and how they will be communicated, thereby forming the foundation of the organization's culture."

Jim agreed with these points and added another. "I would also like to see our stated values included in our quarterly executive team meeting agenda. Let's look at our values and our actions for the prior quarter and make sure we're staying in alignment with them."

"That's fine," Brett responded, "but how are we going to *clearly* communicate your values to the organization?"

"I did the exercise my friend's consultant had them do and took the one hundred values down to my top ten. I could put that in writing and post it on the boardroom wall."

Brett was disappointed in Jim's response. "We agreed a long time ago that we would never post our vision, mission, goals, or values on the wall. We agreed that we would always use language as our method of communication. You know my belief that 'language drives culture.' Let's continue to communicate our values in our meetings and then in frequent communications as opportunities arise in the future. How does that sound?"

Jim appreciated Brett's taking them back to their priorities. It was another sign of a great second-in-command. He agreed and poured more wine for the two of them.

Jim kicked back while enjoying a swallow of wine and summarized the discussion. "So if we've got this right, the first-in-command is responsible for defining the values of the organization, and the second-in-command is responsible for communicating how these values translate to the day-to-day operations. The first- and second-in-command have to have frequent communication with the employees about those values and the behaviors to support the values.

"Couldn't have said it better myself," said Brett.

Jim and Brett gave a toast to each other for the quality of discussion and to a great first- and second-in-command model. They were on a roll. The picture was becoming more and more focused as each critical factor was uncovered and dissected to understand how a first-in-command and second-in-command could successfully form this all-important partnership.

The steak dinner and red wine were making them sleepy, so they both agreed that a good night's sleep would do them good. As they left for bed, Brett reminded Jim that he would get up early the next morning to take a bike ride before continuing their search for what made the noise go away.

Aligning with Owner Values

First-in-Command Duties

- Define the values of the organization.

- Give clarity to the second-in-command of the vision of leadership and the behaviors he expects to see as normal.

Second-in-Command Duties

o   Communicate how these values translate to the day-to-day operations of the organization.

o   Meet with the rest of the organization to communicate the values that will form the desired culture.

Chapter 9

REFLECTING OVER COFFEE

J IM WAS AN EARLY riser, and the next morning was no exception. He woke up and made a pot of strong coffee to kick things into gear. The morning was overcast and cool. Rain was in the forecast, but none had fallen yet. Jim reflected on how the discussions had gone thus far and how powerful the first- and second-in-command principles they were uncovering would continue to be for his business. He felt very fortunate that his business was allowing him the benefits of business ownership. Just three years earlier he had been working seventy-plus hours a week and thinking about the business every hour he wasn't working. The business controlled his thoughts, his emotions, and his life. He had not been told how frustrating business ownership could be, and even if he had he wouldn't have believed it. He had thought financial and physical freedom were guaranteed when he'd invested in the business. Never in his wildest dreams had he realized that he'd be held hostage to the demands of employees, suppliers, clients, his banker, and profits.

He realized that the last couple of years had been much better due to Brett's arrival. But now he had even more clarity about what was happening in his business. Going through the details of what had made the noise go away gave him even more freedom. It would help Brett be even more purposeful at making the noise go away for him and bring great focus to both of them.

The next few hours would be intense. They both struggled with meetings in general, but long meetings were even more difficult. But Jim was encouraged. What they had accomplished so far was inspiring, and he wanted to continue with the same vigor. The prior day had seemed to go by very fast, even though they'd put in a lot of hours. Looking at the list of remaining items was exciting to Jim.

- losing sleep
- leading versus doing
- customers
- making the company look good to others
- bringing new ideas
- results

Jim was gaining energy just looking at these items. He was actually getting anxious for Brett to wake up so they could get started. Right then Brett walked in. It was time to get started.

Chapter 10

LOSING SLEEP

B RETT HAD HIS CUP of coffee and was dressed in workout clothes.

"Nice to see you finally got out of bed, Brett. I thought you were going to sleep until noon."

"It's six thirty, Jim! I've been riding my bike for the last forty-five minutes. I guess you forgot I was going for a ride this morning. Everything must happen at the right time and at the right pace. You don't want me firing in on these concepts until I've burned some energy and had my coffee."

The coffee was strong and had a great aroma. The combination of the mountain air and the coffee created a scent that would inspire anyone.

Brett looked at the original list of what made the noise go away for Jim that was on the window next to where Jim stood. "What is this 'you seemed to be losing sleep for me' topic?"

"What a great morning topic, Brett. I didn't even realize this would be a topic until yesterday when you asked me to tell you what made the noise go away. I remembered the day we were at the coffee shop for our Monday morning meeting. You complained that you hadn't slept the night before because you were concerned about something going on in the business. I almost couldn't stop smiling. It was one of the clearer moments of me feeling safe that I've ever had."

Brett was a little shocked and confused by this statement. "So let me get this straight. You feel safe if I lose sleep?"

"No, Brett; I don't want you to lose sleep. I feel safe when you show evidence of caring about the business as much as I do. Losing sleep is only one way of showing it. I have owned this business for sixteen years, and I can't tell you how many times I've watched employees walk out the door at five o'clock on the dot, leaving a huge problem behind for me to solve. I was thinking about the business day and night, and I believe the employees only thought about it during part of the workday at best. It gets frustrating to be a business owner and have the weight of the business on your shoulders alone. You can't demand or expect that your employees care enough to think about the business after hours; that wouldn't be fair, but it sure makes you feel safe when you see someone who does."

Jim continued, "It isn't just losing sleep that makes me feel like you care about the business. When you show emotion about positive and negative results or are passionate about our vision or anguished over the future, it makes me believe you care. As I said before, I don't really want anyone to lose sleep over the business, but I sure need to know someone else cares about it. If I don't think they care as much as me, it gets noisy, and I feel like I have to dig in to make sure someone is thinking."

Brett understood, but he wanted to get some clear takeaways for a first-in-command and a second-in-command. If they were going to repeat this behavior to make the noise go away for Jim in the future, they would need to really get the concept down cold.

Brett thought he could draw the concepts from Jim with some questioning. "Jim, for us to repeat this concept, we need to capture it and make it clear. What would you say are the key attributes of this trait?"

"Thinking of new ideas is one. When you come in with a new idea for the company I know that you care more about it than you would care about just a J-O-B. Also, when you tell me you stayed up at night, though I really don't want you to stay up, I appreciate the after-hours concern. When you come in before me on a lot of days and stay later than others, that gives me confidence as well. I want your work and family life to be balanced like mine is now, but our business doesn't allow for a weekly eight-to-five job. You take it on yourself to be here when you need to be, and that makes me feel safe."

The concept became even clearer to Brett as Jim continued to explain the key behaviors.

Brett challenged Jim more. "What about the first-in-command's responsibilities here? I can see two things you would have to do. The first is to freely give appreciation and praise when you see this behavior and feel safe. An employee would likely want to replicate the effort if they knew you appreciated it. I never knew you felt safe when I lost sleep over the business. I just thought you were making fun of me that day at the coffee shop.

"The second thing you have to do as a first-in-command is not be disappointed or get frustrated if employees don't show the same level of care and dedication to the business. They really don't have to, and they're not paid to care about the business as much as you do. This is a difficult truth to accept, but it is reality. One of the reasons you care so much is that you have to make this work—you aren't very employable anywhere else!"

Jim laughed at this. But he knew he couldn't work for someone else, so he really was pretty unemployable. He had owned a business way too long to work for someone else.

"Some people just need a job to pay the bills," Brett said. "It isn't the same for them. Our culture will be better if you give our employees a break and not expect them to lose sleep over the business. We need them to be fresh. You and I can lose the sleep.

"We need to capture our key points on paper." He wrote the following:

Lose Sleep and Show You Care

First-in-Command Duties

- Give appreciation and praise when you see this behavior and feel safe.

- Don't be disappointed or get

frustrated if employees don't show the same level of care and dedication to the business.

Second-in-Command Duties

o   Give the perception of caring about the business.

o   Be proactive in showing you care.

Chapter 11

MAKING THE COMPANY LOOK GOOD

"Is that rain I'm feeling on my head or are you perspiring over all this talk about the reality of owning a business?" Jim quipped.

"No, I think that rain we were anticipating is finally making its way to the mountains. Thank God—we really need it! The snowmelt is about gone, and we need some moisture to replenish the reservoirs and springs. Let's move our conversation and flip chart inside before the ink smears."

Jim and Brett hurriedly picked up their materials and sought dry shelter in the cabin as the rain began to increase in strength and volume. The large drops hit the quaking aspen leaves, creating their own rhythm and a natural symphony as a backdrop for their work. It would give new energy to their typically short attention spans.

As they settled down from their exodus from the now rain-drenched porch, Jim regained his thought process and reiterated to Brett how he felt when Brett made him look good. Jim went into the details of how making him look good also made the company look good, and how all this "looking good" trickled down to their employees, clients, corporate advisors, and suppliers.

After listening to Jim's extended summary, Brett was reminded of a related experience he'd had while employed as the vice president of operations by a heavy equipment dealer. It seemed like Brett always had an experience that conjured up a story related to their discussion.

Brett began, "I know you've heard a lot of stories about my time at the heavy equipment business, but I just remembered another incident that relates to this issue. The business had been high quality and successful for over sixteen years. The first-in-command certainly didn't have to have an effective second-in-command to continue his success, but in the end he found out what great value a second-in-command could bring to make his noise go away." Just hearing that phrase again brought sweet music to Jim's ears.

"The event was an annual program that the heavy equipment industry held with all the heavy equipment dealers. The National Association of Equipment Dealers would meet with equipment manufacturers, and they would court each other for special distribution deals. The manufacturers would also put on a big convention-style show to introduce new and innovative technology. The event was huge, completely filling the Las Vegas Convention Center facilities or the entire Orlando Convention Center.

"The first convention I attended was in Chicago. We went to many manufacturer events. Due to our lack of proactively managing the relationships with the manufacturers, we were less prepared than our competitors and were perceived by our manufacturers as less attractive. Awards were handed out, and we were not on the list because our performance was not stellar. We met with our manufacturing representatives in back-to-back meetings in hotel suites, but it was obvious something was wrong. One manufacturer was very large and one of the key supplier lines for our dealership. When we entered the room we found our largest local competitor in the room having a discussion with the manufacturer's top people. They were getting drinks for them and treating them like royalty. They pointed to the drinks and food when we asked about the food. It was a punch in the gut because we were the exclusive dealer of the products in our city, and this didn't look good.

"The entire three days were just like this. One blow after another made us wonder what needed to change to make us a stronger player in future years. As the second-in-command I saw a real opportunity to make the first-in-command feel safe. I told him after the last manufacturer's meeting, 'This is the last time we will ever be treated like this at one of these meetings. In the future, they will be treating us like royalty.' He laughed and said he would love to see that happen.

"The following year we made it happen. I was excited about going back the next year because I had set up formal meetings with key suppliers and was prepared to wow them with our dealership. Also, I had forwarded results and new ideas and innovation in our dealership throughout the year to proactively manage the relationships."

Brett continued. "Well, it paid off. We went to the first meeting with a manufacturer for whom we had not been able to do much during the prior year. We expected a rough meeting, but I had put together a custom marketing plan for their products to increase sales. We entered the room, and all the top players were there, primarily because I had requested this in our invitation. They were fairly cool with us at first and seemed to have a hidden agenda.

"I took over the meeting from the beginning and handed out the marketing plan for their products. We went through the charts, graphs, creative marketing pieces, and a really glamorous presentation. The president was the first to speak when we asked for feedback. He said, 'You know, we were planning to fire you today. However, after looking at this plan I believe we would be foolish to discontinue our relationship.' I looked at the first-in-command, and he had a glow that said, 'Yep, I'm one smart first-in-command for having this stuff put together and hiring this second-in-command.'

"Our products had improved somewhat over the prior year but not enough to get a real 'wow' from these manufacturers. The difference we made this year was how well we managed their perception.

"From that point forward, things began to improve," Brett stated with pride. "We won the top award from another manufacturer, which rewarded us with a trip for two couples to go to Switzerland for a week. We ended up winning awards and received recognition in every subsequent manufacturer meeting, and we were wined and dined by every manufacturer who attended.

"The entire trip gave the first-in-command tremendous confidence. Now, this didn't just happen at the event. When we left the meeting the year before, I knew that the first-in-command had to have success at these meetings to have confidence in the business. He was incredibly talented but didn't have the time to do the things I was able to do as a second-in-command. The noise from the business was very loud when he was worried about what the manufacturers thought of him and his company. He had second-in-commands at prior conventions, and, actually, many other employees had attended those meetings. The noise became louder and louder every year when the first-in-command saw the pressure of these events and knew he was the only one who was going to do something between the events.

"As the second-in-command it took two things to make this work. The first was proactive management of those external relationships and showing the power of an effective second-in-command. Those manufacturers were more confident in a company that had strength behind the first-in-command. The second was to track performance standards to meet what those key third-party relationships needed and make sure we performed at the top of those standards. The first-in-command became more and more confident with every third-party relationship that saw a powerful second-in-command in the organization. Pressure was removed as he was no longer the only person leading the organization. I see a large number of second-in-commands who approach this responsibility in a random fashion and don't create the image of being a powerful part of the organization. It doesn't give the third party confidence, and it creates more noise for the first-in-command."

Jim understood what Brett was saying and clearly saw how a second-in-command bringing value would decrease the noise for a first-in-command. As a matter of fact, it was so clear it triggered how he had felt a few months earlier at a national convention he and Brett had attended.

Jim reminded Brett of this experience. "Do you remember when you and I went to Napa last spring for the national convention? That's when the 'make the noise go away' terminology first started between us."

Over two hundred companies were in attendance at the convention. Different companies had been asked to speak on their successful accomplishments. Jim and Brett had been asked to show what they had accomplished in the modeling and branding of their company. The model was Jim's five-year vision for the company. They were in the second year of implementing this plan, and the vision was quickly becoming a reality.

Jim had started the presentation by telling his story of success and how he had reached a place where his life was very noisy. He communicated that the noise kept him from getting things accomplished. It created barriers to time and energy. He introduced Brett as the guy who had made the noise go away.

"I was so proud of you, Brett. I can't tell you how good I felt when I watched you give that presentation. You were telling my story and our story in a way that made me and the company look better than ever. Heck, I was so impressed with how you presented our vision, I wanted to go back and get to work. I stood on the side of the stage while you presented and did everything I could to make it look like I knew what you were saying. It was all I could do to keep the sides of my mouth from hitting my ears. You know, the next day and a half of that conference was a great time. I walked around that convention with great confidence. Everyone was telling me how lucky I was to have you, and they raved at how impressed they were with our plan. You really made us look great.

"Brett, do you see the irony in this? I introduced you as the guy who made the noise go away and then you made more noise go away with how good you made us look. I had more confidence and assurance about our company because the quality of the presentation and your skills as a presenter made everyone in the audience want a guy just like you."

Brett interrupted, "I received quite a few offers that week. I think they might have been serious."

Jim wasn't going to let Brett bask in the compliments right now. Nor was he willing to open the door for Brett to throw out the "I need a raise" comment again. "I know you're a stud and they loved you, but the key here is I was able to really feel safe about the business after I saw how you impressed others by telling them about our business."

Brett was back at the flip chart ready to write. "So you're saying that an effective second-in-command doesn't just perform, they actually have to help the first-in-command and help make the company look good to others. It strengthens our company and increases the performance capabilities of both of us. We both have to be purposeful at finding these opportunities and delivering at a high level when we get them."

Brett heard the message loud and clear and saw the power of this principle in the first- and second-in-command relationship. He picked up the marker and finished writing the first- and second-in-command duties on the flip chart. They both felt really good about what they had captured in this area.

"I think you nailed it, Brett," Jim said. He leaned over the balcony to see a beautiful white-tailed deer walk around the back of the house. "Sure is quiet up here, my friend."

Make the Company Look Good

First-in-Command

- Give the second-in-command opportunities to make the company look good.

- Recognize and show appreciation for the second-in-command when he or she does a good job of making the company look good.

- Realize you have accomplished something when your second-in-command stands out.

Second-in-Command

- Be proactive in finding ways to make the company and the

first-in-command look good.

o   Don't forget who gave you the
opportunity to look good.

o   Create very high-quality
presentations and go overboard
in making the company look
great.

Chapter 12

SPENDING TIME WITH CLIENTS

THE RAIN OUTSIDE HAD stopped, but it had become a bit chilly in the house. Temperatures could drop quickly in the mountains, and Brett was feeling it. He walked over to the fireplace and built a nice fire to warm up the room a little.

Jim was still very focused after the last storytelling session. He was ready to take on the next item.

"Let's take on this issue of you spending time with clients. This is another area I know makes the noise go away. When you visit a client it makes me feel confident that you understand our business and are keeping up with what our clients need."

Brett shook his head. "This topic is bigger than me, Jim. I don't just go see clients. I make sure you and I both see our clients. This is another one of my purposeful strategies I started early in my career at Golden. In my first few months here I had to get in front of clients so I could understand what they did and what we do and could do for them. After going out a few times, I realized you were not getting the requisite face time with our clients. You are the best in the company when you're in front of them, but you just didn't seem to have time. I built a calendar for both of us to schedule client visits on a regular basis. For the last two years the client visits we have together have been from this plan. I've also given your assistant the names of businesses we need you to visit so she could set the appointments."

"I was wondering how all that was managed. It does feel good to have it managed and not even know it's happening. I knew you had something to do with my getting in front of more clients, but I didn't know why. As a second-in-command, should this be your responsibility?"

Brett sat for a few seconds to contemplate this question. "Yes, I think it is my responsibility. You need the noise to go away. It is not your natural talent to organize and manage client visits. It is my unique ability and my responsibility to make sure we stay relevant with our clients. We can't treat seeing our clients on a regular basis like a New Year's resolution—randomly set the goal and then live through the year and see what happens. Heck no! This won't work. We have to be purposeful if we are going to manage our clients effectively."

Jim once again realized how the noise had gone away from him because of the safety Brett provided by being close to the clients and because he was managing his client visits as well. "So is that it? You manage my client visits, and you go see clients on a regular basis. Do you think this covers this topic well enough?"

"No, Jim!" Brett answered in disgust. "This is a lot more complex than client visits. Seeing them is one thing, but understanding and establishing real relationships with them is something completely different. We have made decisions to change our business over the last few years after learning where our clients are struggling—understanding what keeps them awake at night!

"You and I both have played a lot of sports. One of the worst coaches I ever had was an assistant coach on my high school football team. He was one of those guys who had never played the game but acted as if he knew it all. It was very obvious that he didn't. He told us to do things that didn't have a hint of reality. I remember one time when we were working on getting off the line of scrimmage against a defender. He was telling us how easy it was to get past the person and gave us techniques that just didn't work. He lost all credibility with us. He didn't know what he was talking about. We completely stopped listening to him. I'm sure he had some good ideas and coaching techniques that would help, but since he didn't *really* know, we lost faith in him.

"I know that managers and leaders don't have to be able to do every job in the company. That's not what I'm saying here. I don't think a coach has to play or a manager has to do every job before he or she can lead. However, I do believe a leader has to have an understanding of what the person he or she is leading is up against when doing the job. The leader has to have empathy for the challenges and obstacles that frequently invade our work environment. And he or she should have some related experience to bring to bear on those challenges and obstacles. The combination of an individual's natural intelligence, formal education, industry knowledge, and experience are all tools in our personal tool kit that we can apply to solve problems and create innovative ways to improve operations. But it's also important to understand your work environment so you know how and when to apply your personal tool kit to the particular situation.

"Let me give you another example of what I'm talking about. Back when I started in this business a big competitor of ours had a real problem with the sales manager. He was a great guy with a good management background. He had all the skills of an educated manager. Reports, presentation, communication, sales psychology knowledge, process development, relationship management, and leadership were all on his resume and were credible. But he failed in the job because he was not connected to clients. He had never been in front of electrical contractors. He would tell the salespeople and the staff, 'You don't have to be in front of a client to understand what they want or to know how to sell to them!' He believed that you didn't have to be able to do the job to manage or lead it. This belief system has cost him in his career. Salespeople would come to him for advice, and he would give textbook answers and theoretical insights. He was ineffective, and they quickly lost confidence and trust in him.

"Now, I'm not advocating that he should have been able to sell the product to be able to be the sales manager. He is a very smart guy and very talented in business. All he lacked was time in front of clients and prospects to be able to understand them better and be able to guide and direct the team. His lack of understanding the business and the decision makers his people were selling to kept him from having the trust of his people.

"The guy who followed that sales manager became a good friend of mine. Just like the sales manager before him, he had not sold in the industry. He told me that in his first week he overheard a salesperson telling the first-in-command he would never follow a sales manager who hadn't sold a lot of business in their industry. This sales manager immediately took that challenge. He set an objective to do his sales manager job and to rain make and bring in more business than any other salesperson in the company that year. His objective was to get the trust and confidence of his sales team and develop the understanding of what the clients wanted and expected. This was a great strategy. He gave the company more opportunities in the year than any other salesperson.

"The reward came the day the salesperson—the one who had said he would never follow a sales manager who hadn't sold anything—asked the sales manager if he would go with him on a sales call with a prospect. Now, this sales manager was very effective with the sales team and with building a strategy for the company. He knew what the clients expected, and he understood the challenges of the company's prospects. This wasn't easy to accomplish. He had a big job to do at the company. Management activities like plans, meetings, vendor management, program development, and people management were a full-time job. The time to go see clients and prospects wasn't an easy slot to find in the calendar. But it wasn't optional to him. He established a requirement to have a minimum of at least one face-to-face visit and one phone contact with a client and prospect each week. It was purposeful and calculated, and it worked. He brought in business and understood the clients and prospects as well as anyone in the organization!"

Jim jumped in. "I don't care what work role the second-in-command plays in the organization. I can see now that they have to spend time on a regular basis with the clients. If they want to really stretch themselves, they need to spend time with prospects as well. I can see that without knowing clients very well, a first-in-command could create a lot of noise for himself and for others. So what do we need to capture here, Brett?"

Brett had been taking notes. He pulled out the list and wrote on the board.

Spend Time with Clients

First-in-Command Duties

o   Go see clients according to the plan we create.

o   Hold the second-in-command accountable to proactively see clients.

o   Seek to find out what is keeping your clients up at night.

o   Communicate to your employees what you learn from being with clients.

Second-in-Command Duties

o   Build a client visit calendar to make sure we are purposeful in client visits.

o   Communicate to all key managers and salespeople when they are supposed to see the clients.

o   Hold everyone accountable to follow the plan.

o   Go see clients yourself and communicate to the organization what you learn.

Chapter 13

THE SECOND-IN-COMMAND'S KEYS TO SUCCESS

J IM AND BRETT DECIDED to take a break now that the weather had cleared up. They went their separate ways—Brett to the mountain bike trails and Jim to the river to do some fly-fishing.

Brett was excited about getting some mountain biking time. Getting rid of the stress by challenging a mountain was very effective. Usually he was able to clear his mind on the trails as it took a high level of concentration. But today he couldn't get his mind completely focused on the trail because he was so energized by the discussions he and Jim had been having. As he put on his helmet and jumped on his full-suspension mountain bike, he began to review the previous day's discussion swirling around in his head.

When Jim had invited him up to the cabin to dig in and discover why this first-in-command and second-in-command model was working so well, he had been very excited. Doing a great job was important to Brett, but getting clarity around these items so he could be more purposeful in the future was even more stimulating. Thus far the conversation had been very good, and he realized he would be even more effective when they got back to the city. Some of the past success was instinctive due to plain hard work and a little bit of luck. Now he would be able to execute by strategically applying the principles they were uncovering. He had also had a dream of writing a book about the first- and second-in-command relationship, and this retreat was clearly outlining what he would put in a book.

He realized that principles alone wouldn't work without focus on a few things. He decided to work through the items that would guarantee his success back at the office. The first point he realized was that he had to maintain a trusting relationship with Jim. This trust would be protected and reiterated with frequent communication and results. The processes would be in place with the strategies they were developing, but the execution of those strategies was what would cement the relationship of absolute trust they needed.

Discipline was the next item that came to Brett's mind. Discipline was a natural trait for Brett, but he knew that the discipline required to be an effective second-in-command must be high. A second-in-command usually had a job function to do, and he had to perform all the items to help make the noise go away for the first-in-command. This couldn't be accomplished with inefficient management and disorganization.

He had learned early in his career that he could categorize all his activities into three areas:

- Things he wanted to do
- Things he had to do
- Things he should do

The things he wanted to do, like travel, play golf, and other fun things, seemed to happen when he made the time. The things he had to do were also pretty easy. They were items he was compelled to do and always found a way to get done. Things like going to work on time, paying his bills, and completing projects were compelling, have-to-do items for Brett.

The challenge in life for Brett was the "should-do" items. Should-do items are what cause stress and keep most people from being successful. He knew from experience that when he created internal or external accountability around the should-do items, he had less stress and greater results. He decided that he would get the second-in-command takeaways from this session and build a have-to-do accountability model around it. This strategy would help him guarantee his success in the job.

The last item Brett identified on the ride was the need to check with Jim weekly on what was keeping him up at night. No matter what else happened and what else he was working on, managing what kept Jim up at night was critical to Brett's success. Even if it took a phone call when they couldn't meet in person, he had to get this information. He would make sure to not allow this to slip when he returned to Golden to implement with his renewed energy.

When Brett arrived back at the cabin he went straight to the flip chart to record his list of success items.

Brett's Notes:

o   Trust through frequent communication.

o   Execute and get results.

o   Be disciplined to turn critical "should do" items into "have to" items.

o   Make sure to have the What Keeps Jim Up at Night meeting every Friday.

Chapter 14

THE FIRST-IN-COMMAND'S KEYS TO SUCCESS

A S BRETT MANEUVERED HIS way through the challenging and treacherous trails on his mountain bike, Jim decided he'd take some time to partake in one of his favorite pastimes, fishing. Since Brett had joined his team, Jim had taken advantage of every opportunity to practice his fly-fishing and fly tying skills. His cabin was strategically placed between a healthy mountain stream filled with trout and a fairly large lake that gave up some large fish for a seasoned fly-fisherman.

Jim was excited about the clarity he was obtaining through these discussions with Brett. Much of the credit went to the relaxed environment that provided him the ability to focus on the key issues around making the noise go away. He had learned a lot in the discussions thus far; it was mostly a self-discovery process facilitated very effectively by Brett. As Jim readied his newest mayfly imitation, he contemplated his relationship with Brett and reflected on the reality that he actually had a role in making the noise go away and in helping Brett be an effective second-in-command.

When they had planned to come up to the mountains and take on this project, he had thought Brett was making the noise go away on his own. He hadn't thought through how he needed to do something in every area to make this work. The last couple of years had been great, but they hadn't been perfect. Many of the failures were because of Jim's behavior and actions, not Brett's. He remembered missing communication meetings and not following through with clients Brett had asked him to contact. He saw the power of letting Brett make the company look good. He knew that sometimes he needed to back off from the desire to be front and center in presentations so that others would think highly of the company due to broader management and leadership.

He went back over all the items he and Brett had discussed since arriving in the mountains. It amazed him again that every item had a responsibility for him to follow. Fear actually struck him at this realization. How was he going to keep up with all the things he was responsible for doing in this relationship? Heck, he couldn't remember to do the things he was supposed to do in his marriage. How in the world would he keep up with his responsibilities to Brett?

After quite a few casts into the rocks because his focus was not on fishing, he came to the conclusion. He *had* to get the list of items he was responsible for and put the list in his DayTimer. He committed to himself that he would look at this list every day for ninety days. He knew that after looking at each item for ninety days they would become normal behaviors. Jim was confident that he could follow this plan. He had to do it because the life he was living was what he had expected as a business owner. A little focused effort on being a good first-in-command was certainly worth the reward of having an effective second-in-command.

He felt very blessed to have a great guy like Brett in his business and looked forward to many additional years working with him. Then the next thought jumped into his head. "I guess keeping Brett is not a guarantee. I have to make sure I provide an environment for Brett to be successful." He saw how important it was to do everything he could to assist Brett in achieving success in his role. He had already learned that allowing Brett the requisite freedom to do what he did best paid off with large dividends. But he also realized that continuous feedback and frequent communication were keys to keeping things on track. The bottom line was that he had to *focus* and be *purposeful* in all his behaviors as a first-in-command if it was going to work long-term.

After several noncommittal casts toward some ripples in the stream, Jim realized that any fish that would take his poorly presented fly would have to be starving to death or just plain desperate. So he retrieved his fly and decided to focus on presenting the fly to the fish in a manner that didn't make the fly look like an elephant splashing in the stream. His first cast was perfect, and he set a monster trout on his hook. In a moment the noise went away again.

When Jim arrived back at the house he wrote down his thoughts on the flip chart. He wanted to remember his ideas for making the first- and second-in-command relationship work.

Jim's list:

1. Get the list of first-in-command duties and place in daytimer.

2. Review list every day for next ninety days.

3. Help Brett be successful by communicating frequently.

Chapter 15

LEADING VERSUS DOING

B OTH MEN ARRIVED BACK at the house around the same time. They were very energized due to their individual thinking on their biking and fishing excursions. They knew they were close to the end of the search to understand what made the noise go away and were ready to get back to work.

After a few good fish and bike stories, Jim triggered the conversation back to the project. "Hey, buddy, there's one area where I think I still get noise, but I haven't talked to you about it. You're one heck of a good salesman, and you bring us a lot of revenue. But I'm concerned that you could be more productive if you spent more time teaching others to fish versus giving them the fish, if you know what I mean."

Brett was taken aback by the sudden realization that he may have been flawed in making the noise go away for Jim. He asked for clarity. "I guess I can see your point, but help me understand the balance here, Jim. Our sales were very flat when I first came to the company. I felt the need to get agreement from the sales team that my sales strategy would work. They resisted at first, and now they're strongly following our concepts and strategies. I think that the catalyst to these results is my doing a lot of the sales."

Jim realized he had to give more detail to help Brett see what he was talking about. "Don't get me wrong, Brett; you absolutely had to do a lot of selling in the beginning to become the true sales leader. But I've felt concern that you're working too many hours and spending too much time on individual selling. I don't think you could ever stop selling, but I would like to see you spend more time teaching the other salespeople how to sell. If we can get all our salespeople to sell as well as you, we'll realize a tremendous amount of growth."

These words gave Brett an ego boost, but he was still trying to reconcile his thoughts. He had evolved into spending quite a bit of time doing direct sales. Had he evolved into doing too much and not leading enough?

The look on Brett's face gave Jim a sense that he was struggling with what he was saying. "Brett, let me give you a little more insight. A couple of years ago I was at a business owner network meeting with eleven other owners. Our conversation that day was about productivity. I found it very interesting that every owner in the room said they had productivity concerns because most of the managers in their firms didn't have time to lead and manage their people. They said their managers had evolved into doing a J-O-B and just didn't have the time for people. I think this is a common phenomenon. Most promotable people are very good at doing high-performance things in the company. Sometimes getting results through others is slow and not as quickly rewarding. I can see how anyone would want to go get some immediate results.

"When those business owners expressed that their managers did not have the time to manage people, I found it very ironic that almost all of them were hired to manage people, but they had allowed themselves to evolve into doing a job versus leading others to do the job. This clearly eliminates the advantage of having someone lead. I'm not saying you were one of these people back then. Back when that meeting occurred, you *had* to do more of the selling because you needed to develop a reputation and credibility with the team. But I think that time has passed and you have all the credibility you need. The team supports you, and they believe in your ability and methods. I'm not saying you've done anything wrong at this point, but I believe you need to begin to shift your efforts more toward helping others sell as opposed to doing it yourself."

Brett saw the picture clearly at this point. "I see what you're saying, Jim. I love the sale, and the results motivate me. I have to continue to stay in the game, but we'll be better off if I shift more of my efforts toward helping other salespeople sell, and you will feel safe. You're right on the mark with this one, Jim. I can't believe I let it get to this point."

Jim didn't want Brett to be too hard on himself. "Hey, I appreciate the sales and the results. Your efforts have been a tremendous catalyst to our growth. However, it's time to move these same results to the rest of the team."

"Okay, Jim; let's do it. So the make-the-noise-go-away item for me is to balance my workload to make sure to get my team to increase performance and balance the amount I do versus how much I lead. I have to say that I need you to do something for me as well."

Jim hadn't thought about how he could help, so he was all ears.

"I need you to encourage me and keep me focused on this. It's my natural instinct to go get those results. I'll be driven to get the sales *now* and may fall right back into this model quickly. It's natural, you know. If you said that all the CEOs at your meeting told you their managers had fallen into this trap, I would guess it's natural for most of us. So, as the first-in-command, I need you to encourage me and hold me accountable to lead versus do a job."

Jim liked what he heard and realized he had a role in this principle, as he did in all principles. "Absolutely, Brett; I can do that. Let's make sure to add yours and my responsibilities in this area to our chart."

Brett wrote on the flip chart.

Lead Versus Do

First-in-Command Duties

- Communicate when the second-in-command is doing versus leading.

- When the second-in-command wants to get quick results, encourage him to be patient and train others.

Second-in-Command Duties

o   Lead versus do a job.

o   Don't let your ego get in the way and want to do things yourself

o   Be purposeful in training and developing others to perform.

Chapter 16

BRINGING NEW IDEAS

B RETT LOOKED BACK FROM the board after writing the second-in-command duties and smiled. "Hey, we're on the last two topics! I think we're getting close. Why don't you give your thoughts on this Bringing New Ideas principle?"

"Certainly," Jim answered. "I think this is an important one for making the noise go away. I have struggled for years with this one. Do you have any idea how many nights I've spent at home thinking and believing that I was the only person who would bring a new idea to our business? It gets lonely, frustrating, and a little scary to think you're the only one who will come up with ways to improve the business.

"Since arriving, Brett, you've put in new performance management systems, designed and implemented our corporate marketing plan, built our sales system, increased controls for our inventory, put training programs in place, improved our internal processes, and more. Nobody else in the history of this company has brought this many new ideas and strategies to this company, other than myself of course. You have contributed great value.

"Most of my peers complain they don't have anyone else bringing new ideas to the business. I can see where a second-in-command could fall into the role of just executing a first-in-command's ideas, but you've done a great job of thinking about how we can be a better company and implementing those ideas. These may seem like standard, expected things a second-in-command should do, but based on my experience and the experience of other first-in-commands, you're an exception.

"You've made a huge impact, but you may remember it didn't start out that great. Do you remember when you came to me and said you were going to stop bringing new ideas because I rejected everything?"

Brett remembered this well. He had been so frustrated that he was about to go find another job. "Yeah, I remember. You were driving me crazy."

Jim continued. "Well, remember that the reason I wasn't accepting your ideas was because you weren't bringing those ideas to me in the proper manner. You were bringing me the idea along with all the reasons we should do it. You were so mad that day. What did you call me again?"

Brett started laughing. "I called you Mr. Find Something Wrong with Everything. It was so frustrating to present an idea to you."

"Well, it's a good thing we were able to talk and understand why that was happening. I had to identify all the negative sides of the idea since you were only bringing the positives ones to me."

Brett tried to defend himself again. "I know it came across that way, but I was just trying to sell you."

Jim didn't want to lose the success from that day, so he reminded Brett of what they had decided. "I hear you, and your intentions were good, but we agreed that just presenting one side of an idea would require me to verbalize and think about the other side of it. That forced me to find the negative aspects. We agreed that you would bring me the good and the bad of every idea and we would come to a decision with the best consequence, like you do so well now."

Brett nodded his head. "You accept almost all my ideas since we changed that model. I guess it has worked well since then, and you're not such a downer anymore." They both laughed.

Jim continued his thoughts. "This bringing new ideas thing is big. You've brought a lot of great ideas to the company, and we're much better off because of it."

"I don't know if I'm correct in this theory, but I've always felt that someone who's an owner or potential owner of a company has to bring perceived and recognizable value to the company. The only way I know to measure that is to judge whether a buyer would pay more money for the business if that person was in the company or if they contributed something that someone was willing to pay more to get. As my second-in-command and someone who will be earning ownership in the company at some point, I would expect that you should bring that kind of value. When you bring new ideas and make positive changes to our business I believe you're building a value position for you and our company. This is valuable for both of us."

Brett knew he was doing a good job of bringing new ideas, but he didn't want it to be random and something that became the last priority in his job. He had plenty to do every day, and it would be easy for him to fall into the same situation as the unsuccessful second-in-commands Jim had mentioned earlier. He walked over to the middle of the porch and faced the big window. He looked at the reflection of the mountain and trees while thinking about how to maintain success in this area.

Jim could see he was in deep thought. "So what's on your mind there, buddy?"

"I don't want to be one of those other second-in-commands who get so busy they can't come up with new ideas or don't have time to implement them."

Jim was not as concerned as Brett because he felt Brett would do this naturally, but he felt the need to help. "What do you do now to make sure you're bringing new ideas?"

"Well, first of all I'm passionate about our success and know we have to look to new ideas and strategies if we want to survive. I don't think that's any different from most second-in-commands. I'm pretty focused on having my monthly planning review sessions. This is where most of my new ideas or implementation strategies are developed."

"Okay." Jim saw an opening to move Brett forward. "Tell me about those sessions."

"As you know, we do our strategic planning annually, and we review it quarterly as a management team. But every month I take a day and review all of our objectives and plans and think about how we can improve upon what we're doing. I don't bring every new idea to you because most of them are tweaks to make sure our plan is executed. If I think we need to go a different direction or if something requires unbudgeted capital, I bring the idea to you. Of course, I bring both positive and negative consequences to the new ideas. This is the only way I know of to stay on top of getting the results we have to have."

"I think you just solved your own dilemma, Brett. You have a process and it works. I have to believe one day per month of working on the business like that is great use of your time. Plus it will make sure new ideas and strategies are introduced and executed. I don't think you need to do anything different."

Brett wanted to keep the momentum going, so he took the marker and wrote on the board.

Bringing New Ideas

First-in-Command Duties

- Challenge and encourage the second-in-command to come up with new and innovative ideas.

- Require the second-in-command to bring both positive and negative consequences related to the new ideas.

- Publicly recognize and reward new ideas and show appreciation.

Second-in-Command Duties

- Always think about ways to improve the business.

o   Don't "sell" ideas to the first-in-command using a one-sided approach; rather, present both sides using the consequence decision making approach.

o   Be proactive at bringing value to the business.

o   Hold a monthly strategy session to look at current plans and think of ways to improve what you are doing.

Chapter 17

BRINGING RESULTS

J IM SAW THE ONLY item left on the list and was highly inspired to take it on. "RESULTS!" he screamed out. "Brett, do you remember when you first started and I said your performance objectives are very simple ... execution or execution?"

Brett shook his head with disgust. "Yes, I remember when you told me that. It was really cute. Does it surprise you as much as it surprises me that I'm still here?"

Jim laughed. "The bottom line of a good second-in-command is results. I guess the name of the game for having a strong second-in-command is that we both must focus on getting results. The structure we've built allows for great results. We can focus on our unique abilities and talents. The noise is gone, and I'm not getting in your way. This is a great formula for both of us to achieve high-level results. So how do we assure ourselves of getting those results?"

Performance management was one of Brett's real strengths, so this was a topic he could jump on with confidence. "Results will happen if we continue to follow the principles we've outlined. That is not a concern. The concern I have is whether we're focused on the right results. We have to have clear expectations of what we expect from each other, and then we have to be accountable to do what we say we will. It's a simple process, but we have to be consistent in the application of the principles and disciplined to carry them through."

Jim agreed with Brett's assessment. "So how do we do this, and how do we set those expectations?"

"We have to take out the trash." Brett leaped from his chair and threw a piece of trash in the garbage can across the porch.

"Nice shot, buddy. That was impressive! Now, what the heck do you mean we have to take out the trash?"

Brett stood up and began speaking as if he were presenting to a crowd. "I've told you about my father. One of the greatest lessons I've learned and applied in my business career was directly related to an experience with him.

"I can remember this incident like it was yesterday. My father yelled across the house, 'Brett Giles, get down here *now*.' I had heard those words before, and I knew this wasn't good.

"I had a tendency to create excitement with my parents as a self-involved fourteen-year-old boy. Most of the time I didn't have a clue as to why he was yelling for me, but this time I was pretty sure. Going down the stairs, I was preparing a good answer to why I had, once again, failed to take out the trash.

"I arrived in the kitchen, where my six-foot-seven-inch two-hundred-and-fifty-pound ex-professional football player father was standing. He's normally a kind man, but he was upset that I hadn't taken out the trash … again. With my busy schedule living the life of a highly social athlete, student, and playboy—I thought—I frequently forgot that I was responsible for certain chores around the house, specifically taking out the trash.

"Dad started the discussion with a more controlled tone than usual. He said that the yelling, groundings, and many other punishments had had little to no effect on me, and he was ready to try a new angle. His tone was soft but direct. 'Son, I don't know how many times I've told you to take out the trash, but I'm sure getting tired of repeating myself with no results.' I can imagine how hard it was for him to refrain from just putting me headfirst into the trash can to bring home the point. He elaborated, 'We can't continue to have these discussions. It is your job to take out the trash, clean your room, and help your mother with other miscellaneous cleaning. I expect you to do those things without constant reminders, and I am going to go to extreme measures of punishment if you don't start doing your job.' My mind began racing about what this new punishment could possibly be. Funny thing—instead of setting my mind on remembering to put out the trash in the future, I immediately considered the possible alternative punishment methods for not putting out the trash. But then again, I was fourteen. I digress ...

"Don't forget, six-foot-seven, two hundred and fifty pounds, and I was certain he could crush my head in the palm of his hands. He was clearly getting my attention now.

"He informed me that he was going out of town for the next three days and when he returned he would check to see if I had completed all my chores, confirming with Mom that I had taken the trash out every day. He assured me the consequences would be severe if I didn't take out the trash. Head crushing was my fear, even though he would never physically hurt me. Then he left town.

"At that point he had completely gained my attention and focus. He had made the point very clear, and I was certain that he needed me to be impressed. I've always been a little bit of a salesman, so I decided to sell Dad on what a great son I was.

"So ... I started to work. The next day—a fourteen-year-old guy has to rest, you know—I began my quest to impress. I looked around the house for great things to do to impress my father. I found a high-profile opportunity to gain favor. The backyard had a ton of leaves on the ground, as many as you could have in west Texas. I went to work cleaning up every single leaf.

"While cleaning the leaves out of the bushes, I noticed that the wood window seals were in need of repainting. I began the next job of sanding and painting the trim around the windows. This seemed to be working well, so I took off the rest of the day.

"When the next day arrived I decided a little more work would be worth it to possibly get me a good two to three months of appreciation from Dad. I did some vacuuming around the house and a few more miscellaneous items that were clearly what was necessary to seal the deal of praise from Dad.

"So, day three arrives ... Dad comes in the front door. I'm in my room waiting for him to break into the hallelujah chorus. Unfortunately, the chorus sounded something like this: 'Brett Giles, get your butt down here right now.' It was at this point, with my keen ability to determine where he was standing when yelling through the house, that I realized he was standing next to the trash can. I forgot to take out the trash!

"Oh my gosh, my heart sunk into my tennis shoes. I could barely lift my feet to move toward the stairs. It was not an issue of whether he was going to kill me or not; it was an issue of *how* he would kill me. As I *slowly* walked down the stairs I tried to think of how to get out of this one.

"It came to me. How in the world could he be mad at me with all the extra work I had done? He probably wouldn't even be mad. He'd probably get to that hallelujah chorus he was unable to sing in the beginning. Maybe I could ask for some money or a nice gift. This was going to be better than I thought. I sped up.

"When I reached the kitchen I saw the fire in his eyes. I felt it best to stay out of his reach until I could explain what a model son he had. He looked at the trash can and said, 'Did I not ask you to take out the trash while I was gone? You not only didn't take it out every day, you didn't take to out one time. I can see the same trash in here that I left three days ago.'

"I decided it was time to interrupt and begin the self-promotion that would lead to great praise. I told him that I knew I was supposed to take out the trash and then asked him to wait until he heard what I did. I went through the laundry list of wonderful results I had accomplished over the previous three days.

"He listened to me and looked at me like I had lost my mind. He's a very wise man and very intelligent. He allowed me to finish my huge list of wonderful work, and then he taught me one of the greatest business lessons I would ever learn.

"He told me that it was great that I had done so many extra things, but it didn't meet the minimum requirement, or the objectives, for our family, like a business, to be successful. He said that our house had some basic results for us to accomplish or we would fail, go out of business. These desired results were assigned to each family member and if any one of us didn't do our job, we would have problems. He continued to tell me that my not taking out the trash had a bad consequence of the kitchen smelling bad and bugs and other problems follow unclean environments.

"He said that doing those extra chores could never overcome the failure to do the basics, like take out the trash. He then told me that he wished I hadn't done some of the extra activities. The leaves were protecting the grass, which we were trying to grow in the desert, from the winter weather. I had to go put them back down, by the way. He suggested that after taking out the trash it would have been best for me to clean the garage. This would have helped organize our house and would have been a great benefit to our family.

"What did I learn? You have to have *clear* expectations for every person in the company, and you have to help them understand why they are doing them. The expectations seemed clear to me with my father. The problems were that between the communication and execution, I forgot what I was supposed to do and I didn't have clarity of why I was doing it. Expectations become clear when there is no doubt what someone is supposed to do, why they are doing it, and how it will be measured, and when other distractions are eliminated from the expectations. That includes you and me, Jim. Those expectations have to be based on the core attributes that will bring the most value to the success of the business. Both of us know what we need to do, but we both have had a tendency to get caught up doing less important stuff.

"I also learned something else as I reflected on this event in later years. You know how you feel when an employee comes to you during a review, or sometime during the year, and tells you that they did 'so many extra items' that they want and deserve a raise or promotion? You look at them and think 'you did extra things, but you didn't do your job, or take out the trash,' and you want to fire them? The day my father and I had this discussion, I was clear about what my father wanted me to do, but I didn't understand the big picture of what needed to be done for our family's success and what my role was in the big picture.

"This is a common problem in business because most employees don't know what is expected of them or how their role fits into the big picture. When they don't have clarity of what is expected, they'll do whatever they think will make them look good for praise and promotion. So you and I need to build our expected results and make a commitment to hold each other accountable to 'take out the trash.'"

It was easy for Jim to agree to this concept, as he was scattered at best in his approach to work. Knowing that he would have clarity about what he needed to do to bring the greatest results was empowering and made more of the noise go away. "When are we going to get these objectives for you and me written?"

Brett said he would make it a priority on Monday when they were back at work. Both men really felt good about this clarity. They knew it would keep them both focused and the results would be powerful to the company.

Jim wanted to hear the end of the story from Brett. "What happened with your father and you after he taught you the lesson?"

"Well, obviously he didn't kill me, as you can see. That event did have pretty severe consequences. We did something pretty neat after that experience. Our entire family sat down and developed a positive and negative reward system. Each person in the family had to do standard items as a base for our performance. We had a chalkboard in our garage where we checked off our regular chores to show we had completed them. We had an additional list of chores that we did and got paid for doing them. They brought additional value to the family so my parents were willing to pay us for doing them. We also had clear consequences for not doing our chores. I won't go into the details of those consequences. I can tell you that they were progressive in nature, and they were motivating enough to get us back on track when we didn't do our chores."

"So how does this work for us?"

"Well, we just developed the process. I guess we need to develop the positive and negative rewards. You started this discussion with the statement 'execution or execution.'" Brett liked the rhyme and discipline of this statement, but they both knew they wouldn't fire Brett if he fell slightly short on one or two items. Brett continued his thoughts. "What kinds of positive and negative rewards do you want to put in place?"

Jim walked across the porch while he contemplated his answer. Then he spoke. "Why don't we do something similar to what your family did? We'll have our list of primary objectives from the process we just developed. If we fall short we could have a financial consequence. I don't want to take money away from either of us, but maybe reduce our bonuses based on chore execution. Then we could build additional bonus opportunities for additional work that goes above and beyond the core responsibilities."

Brett liked the idea, but the approach made him feel somewhat selfish. He knew he would reach his objectives and would most likely exceed them. He wanted to spread the rewards to others who were contributing in the company and thought of an idea. "What if we put the extra bonus money in a reward pool for other employees? We don't have to tell them where it's coming from, but we could have some additional money available to randomly reward people when they take out the trash and go above and beyond. This could be fun, and it would be very motivating to me."

Jim loved the idea and gave Brett the go-ahead to put that in place. This discussion really added value to the whole results focus.

Brett grabbed the marker again and wrote on the board.

Results

First-in-Command Duties

o Be accountable to the second-in-command to do what you say you will do.

o Work to do more than what is expected to build a pool of dollars for employee recognition rewards.

o Be clear on what is expected of the second-in-command, and make sure he knows why he is doing it.

o Hold the second-in-command accountable.

Second-in-Command Duties

o *Hold the first-in-command accountable for doing what he says he will do.*

o *Be accountable to the first-in-command to do what you say you will do.*

o *Work to do more than expected to build a pool of dollars for employee recognition rewards.*

o *Build the clear performance objectives for the first- and second-in-command based on your annual strategic plan.*

After inking the final bullet on the flip chart, it hit them both that they were actually finished. They had done it! They were finished with the project. Jim was thrilled with what they accomplished over the weekend. It was more than he had expected. He and Brett had new clarity about their roles and responsibilities, and Jim had even less noise than when he'd arrived. Both of them realized they had uncovered something most business people in the world would never know: how to make the noise go away.

Chapter 18

HIRING AN EFFECTIVE SECOND-IN-COMMAND

A COUPLE OF MONTHS after the mountain trip to Jim's cabin, Brett entered Jim's office. It was early on a Monday before the weekly communication meeting, and Jim was reading.

"Hey, Jim, how was your weekend? Mind if I pick your brain for a couple of minutes?" Brett and Jim had decided that Brett would take the concept of making the noise go away and go after his goal of writing a book.

"Yeah, sure. What's on your mind?"

"I'm trying to get the final structure for the book, and I think we're missing something. We created clarity around what the first- and second-in-command must do in the relationship. But if I was a first-in-command and read this book, and didn't have a second-in-command, I would want your advice on what I should look for when hiring a second-in-command."

Jim nodded. "I think if I was a current or future second-in-command, I would also want to know that information. Yeah, sure; I can give you some thoughts."

Brett sat in the chair across the room and pulled out his notepad. "Tell me what you would look for if you were to replace me. Oh, and don't get any big ideas about doing that either."

Jim laughed. "Many of my friends ask me how to find an effective second-in-command. They also ask what attributes they should look for. After our retreat in the mountains, I've had numerous first-in-commands ask me about what we accomplished. After telling them the details, many of them have asked me what they should look for when hiring a second-in-command. Let me get my notes.

"Number one, communication skills. An effective second-in-command should have the natural ability to be proactive in communicating so they can follow the first principle of making the noise go away.

"Number two, intelligence. The second-in-command must be smart enough to work in the industry and understand what everyone in the business does. I would also want to see signs of good business acumen. Does the candidate have the good business judgment to make us a better company?

"Number three. Doesn't have to be a future first-in-command. A second-in-command might eventually evolve to become a first-in-command, but the best second-in-commands I've seen are lifelong second-in-commands. They have a passion to help others succeed and want to serve in that role. This is a tough issue. If perpetuation is a big need, the potential of becoming a first-in-command should be one of the factors considered.

"Number four. A second-in-command should like spending time with clients. He or she cannot be effective if he or she doesn't enjoy being around the client. We talked about this in the list of things that a second-in-command must do to make the noise go away. But I would want to see this behavior in prior business experiences. Client contact and involvement are not things you just start later in your career. You either like to do it and make it happen or you don't.

"Number five, they must have strong presentation skills. A critical element of making the first-in-command feel safe is how the second-in-command presents the company to others.

"Number six, the second-in-command should have unique abilities complementary to the first-in-command. Not necessarily strengths matching weaknesses, but the requirement here is to fill in skills that either complete or complement the first-in-command's or other organizational needs.

"Number seven, strong strategic planning skills. Strategic

planning can help the organization reach objectives more quickly, and it really makes the noise go away for me. It helps with prioritizing the ideas I have and keeping us focused on our priorities.

"Number eight, I think an effective second-in-command would be very good at organizing thoughts, ideas, and processes. Organizing ideas, materials, thoughts, and meetings lines up with having strong strategic planning skills as well.

"Number nine, effective second-in-commands should be able to handle complexity. They must be able to manage multiple items at a time and have a minimum of one year of clear visioning skills. Without this complexity, I don't think they could manage to keep all the balls in the air that are required to do the job, and I don't think they could see far enough into the business future to be effective.

"And finally, number ten, an effective second-in-command has to be named Brett. I can't think of anyone who is more equipped to make the noise go away!" They both laughed.

Brett loved the list and was excited about taking these items and building a hiring process for a second-in-command.

A few weeks later Brett walked into Jim's office and asked him if he would give feedback on the second-in-command hiring formula. Jim was thrilled to see it but not surprised that Brett had done the work.

Brett left it on his desk and asked him to review it and give him feedback.

Jim jumped right into the document. He knew it would be very valuable to any first-in-command.

The Second-in-Command Hiring Formula™

Principle: A second-in-command holds a complex job and should not be hired based on secondhand information or a single interview. Analyzing a second-in-command requires a complex method, but this tool is simplified with a step-by-step process.

Hiring Theory: A high-quality second-in-command will not respond well to the master-slave style of management or interviewing. A second-in-command will be in a peer to peer relationship with a first-in-command at some point, and should be treated that way in the hiring process. Sitting across the desk with supervisor-subordinate-style questions will be offensive to many second-in-commands. Go through the process in the same way you want to work with that second-in-command. Get out from behind the desk and learn as much about what the candidate has done as what he or she says he or she will do. A person's past will give you a lot of clarity about what he or she will do for you.

Depending on the organization, you will follow the hiring process individually or with a team. The more complex the organization, the more people you will want involved in the interviews and evaluation. Some of these steps can be combined if appropriate for you and the candidate.

Process Summary:

Attracting Possible Candidates: Don't wait until you are ready to hire to start looking for a second-in-command. Treat hiring a second-in-command like finding an ideal client. Have a prospect list of potential hires. Keep your eyes open for people in the market who might be a good fit. Keep in touch with these prospects, and be ready to pull the trigger when you are ready.

First Step: Initial meeting. Meet the person and show him or her your company. Give him or her a clear picture of your company and what he or she would be joining. Let the candidate get to know you, and give him or her clarity about your hiring process and how it works. Let the candidate know that it is an extensive process and it is not a quick decision for either of you. Give an executive briefing of the company. This is an early sell, but you should be observing behavior and looking to see how the potential hire takes what he or she learns and applies it through the process. Get his or her agreement to go through the process.

Second Step: Formal interview. Experience-based interviews are best for a second-in-command. Don't ask what he or she is going to do; ask what he or she has done. Ask how he or she handled situations and circumstances. Ask how he or she dealt with situations you have had to see how he or she thinks. Questions should begin with phrases like "Tell me how you handled ... " or "In your current position, what ... " or "What is your best success story?" or "What has been your biggest failure and how did you handle it?"

Third Step: Presentation interview. Ask the potential second-in-command to give you a presentation on his or her goals and what it takes to reach those goals. This will give you clarity on the candidate's future plans and will show you his or her ability to present.

Fourth Step: Reverse interview. This is an opportunity for the potential candidate to ask questions about your firm. You will learn about the candidate's question-asking skills and thought process.

Fifth Step: Develop a success plan for the second-in-command. This plan will include performance objectives, training, compensation, goals, and support structure for one to three years. A candidate has to know the path he or she will take to success.

Sixth Step: Develop the financial offer and present the plan and financial package. Put a deal together that will allow for your organization to grow with this second-in-command. Pay for performance is typically how a second-in-command will want to be compensated. An annual review with a percentage raise will not attract a strong candidate. Your offer should be collaborative in presentation. Stay in the peer-to-peer relationship mode rather than a superior-subordinate relationship. This model will allow for better dialogue and openness for both of you while making the decision.

You are looking for the following attributes in this interview:

1. Communication skills. An effective second-in-command needs the natural ability to be proactive in communicating in order to follow the first principle of making the noise go away.

2. Intelligence. The second-in-command must be smart enough to work in the industry and understand what everyone in the business does. I would also want to see signs of good business acumen. Does the candidate have the good business judgment to make you a better company?

3. The second-in-command doesn't necessarily need to have high potential as a first-in-command. A second-in-command might eventually evolve to become a first-in-command, but the best second-in-commands I've seen are lifelong second-in-commands. He or she has a passion to help others succeed and to serve in that second-in-command role. This is a tough issue. If perpetuation is a big need, the potential of becoming a first-in-command should be one of the factors considered.

4. A second-in-command should like spending time with clients. A second-in-command cannot be effective if he or she doesn't enjoy being around the client. We talked about this in the list of things that a second-in-command must do to make the noise go away. But

I would want to see this behavior in prior business experiences. Client contact and involvement is not something you just start later in your career. You either like to do it, and make it happen, or you don't.

5. He or she must have strong presentation skills. A critical element of making the first-in-command feel safe is how the second-in-command presents the company to others.

6. He or she must have unique abilities complementary to the first-in-command. Not necessarily strengths matching weaknesses, but the requirement here is to fill in skills that either complete or complement the first-in-command or other organizational needs.

7. He or she should have strong strategic planning skills. Strategic planning can help the organization reach objectives more quickly, and it really makes the noise go away for me. It helps with prioritizing the ideas I have and keeping us focused on our priorities.

8. He or she should be very good at organizing thoughts, ideas, and processes. Organizing ideas, materials, thoughts, and meetings lines up with strong strategic planning skills as well.

9. He or she should be able to handle complexity. The candidate must be able to manage multiple items at a time and have a minimum of one year of clear visioning skills. Without this complexity, I don't think he or she could manage to keep all the balls in the air that are required to do the job, and I don't think he or she could see far enough into the business future to be effective.

10. He or she should be experienced at managing and leading people. He or she must have experience with getting things done through others and following HR principles.

Jim reviewed the hiring plan and felt the tool was outstanding. He gave it back to Brett and told him he wouldn't change a thing. He did mention that his advice would be to give a second-in-command the list of items it takes to be a successful second-in-command. Brett reminded him the book would be written for first and secon-in-commands to read.

Chapter 19

THE AWAKENING

IT HAD BEEN OVER six months since Jim and Brett had arrived home from the mountains. Jim was seeing even greater results from Brett now that they were purposeful in executing the strategies they'd realized on their retreat. Jim couldn't be happier with the results and felt like the noise had truly gone away.

Jim was heading to a lunch appointment with a good friend who was a retired vice president of a large general contracting company. His name was Mike Elliot. He didn't know that this lunch would provide the final piece of the puzzle of how to make the noise go away.

The lunch discussion quickly traveled to the retreat in the mountains and the development of the principles to make the noise go away. Jim spoke with excitement and passion as he described all the topics and some of the stories that accompanied the strategy. Mike was very interested but had a look of frustration and almost disgust with the topic.

Jim finally asked about his friend's reaction. "Mike, you don't seem to like the discussion we're having. What's up?"

Mike was surprised that Jim had so quickly picked up on his negative body language. Mike realized he needed to explain himself.

"Jim, I used to be Brett. I don't know if I was really as good as you've described Brett, but I know my CEO felt the same way you do. He was enjoying the fruits of being an owner. He had time to do what he loved to do, was coaching his kids' teams, and was only involved in the things in the business where he was uniquely talented. He was living a great life and truly enjoyed having a strong second-in-command."

Jim was confused. "So why is this a problem for you, Mike?"

Mike responded in stride. "It's not a problem for me. It's a problem for my old boss because he doesn't have me as a second-in command any longer. His life has gone back to what it was prior to my coming on board. He took me for granted, and it finally became an environment completely built around him. I had no choice but to leave. All I could think about when you were talking about how well Brett was performing was how long you'll keep him."

When Mike's words finally sunk in, Jim nearly panicked. Now he had the same blank stare in his eyes, and Mike could see that what he had just said had really hit home. He felt his stomach tie up in knots.

"What would I do if Brett left?" Jim thought. He had assumed Brett would be with him forever. He immediately wondered if he was at risk of losing Brett. He wanted to understand what had happened to Mike so he could avoid the same negative outcome. In near desperation, he asked Mike, "Please, tell me what happened to make you want to leave."

Mike was happy to share what had happened to him because he liked Jim and Brett. He was willing to do what he could to help, since he felt guilty for obviously unnerving Jim so. "The guy I worked for was very talented and ran the business very well, at least early on. He had started the company by himself when he was very young and grew the business into a multimillion-dollar operation. But he finally reached a business size that was too much for him to handle. He was employing the same management techniques that he used when he'd started the business, even though he now employed more than a hundred people. He needed someone who could do things better than he could in certain areas.

"One of my greatest strengths was one of the topics you described earlier when you were explaining how effective Brett is at presenting the company to others. A natural ability I have is creating opportunities to make a company shine in the public eye and creating and maintaining key third-party relationships. I orchestrated speaking opportunities all over the country that would highlight the company's abilities. I created media recognition by applying for industry awards and other local recognition, which the company frequently won. My efforts were very successful and very purposeful.

"Unfortunately, my CEO's ego got in the way. Or maybe my ego was in the way. Either way, it ended badly for him and, fortunately, good for me. A second-in-command who delivers at a high level and makes the company look good becomes very attractive to others. At every place I've ever worked as a second-in-command, the first-in-command has been the envy of his peers, and I've been the target of more opportunities than I can count. Don't get me wrong, I was not ever looking or trying to find work and leave. I was very committed to the company. But a strong second-in-command is hard to find, and supply and demand makes it easy to leave if you're not shown the level of appreciation you deserve. I guess a good CEO should love to have a staff full of people who are the envy of others rather than having employees who nobody else wants."

Mike continued, "I started seeing articles written about the company that highlighted great things I was doing but giving all the credit to the first-in-command. These were interviews with the first-in-command that I was setting up for him. The first-in-command didn't even know when I was speaking at certain events, and when he did know, he didn't even ask how the event went. He was taking me for granted. Looking at the success of the company, he was convinced it was due only to his efforts. I know he contributed, but I felt it was a team of people who were contributing.

"I guess when you don't get the appreciation you think you deserve, you go where the appreciation will be plentiful. It didn't take much time or effort to find a new opportunity. I really didn't want to leave, but the CEO's lack of appreciation made a lot of other companies very attractive. I didn't have any problem finding another company that needed or wanted a proven second-in-command.

"When I left the company it immediately became very 'noisy' for the CEO. At first he enjoyed regaining complete control over the business, but he quickly realized how much value I brought and has suffered the consequences for years since. Truth be known, I think he did appreciate me. He just didn't show it. If I were to give advice based on my past experience, I would say the first-and-second-in-command relationship requires that both work to help the other be successful. If you utilize the second-in-command effectively and show appreciation and recognition for what they do, you will find a long-term relationship of 'quiet' because the noise will go away, if you don't mind me using your term."

Jim had a sick feeling in his stomach. "I wonder if Brett feels this way?" he thought. "Do I show him adequate appreciation?" His mind raced back to the retreat at his cabin. During one of his fishing breaks Jim had asked himself: "Have I expressed my sincere appreciation for Brett's contribution? Have I told him how much I depend on him, how much I trust him, and just how much I appreciate all the time and energy he has put into helping me reshape my company?"

Jim knew instantly what he had to do. He turned to Mike with a new look of determination and thanked him for sharing his experience and opening his eyes to a potential disaster.

"I can't lose him," Jim thought. He called Brett on his cell phone and asked to meet him in a few minutes.

Jim rushed to the office. Brett sat at the conference table. Jim began the meeting with a very direct conversation. He told him about his meeting with Mike and his experience as a second-in-command. He wanted to know if Brett had any of these feelings. Brett's response surprised him.

"Well, Jim, I guess I'm glad we're having this conversation. It shows me how much you appreciate me and gives me confidence in our trust and relationship. Just like a NFL quarterback wants to finish his career with the team he starts with, I want to stay here. But I know neither of us can take that for granted. It is something we have to work on and maintain."

Jim sat up quickly, ready for any clarity it took to make sure they would work together for a long time. He was not going back to the way things had been before Brett. "Okay, what do we need to do to make sure we work together for the rest of our careers?"

Brett answered like he had planned the meeting himself. "I can think of a few things, Jim. At the end of the day all any employee really wants is to be treated fairly. An employee has to be viewed and valued in the supply and demand model. The reason I've been with three companies in my career is because the supply of good second-in-commands is low and the demand is high. Someone else is usually willing to do more to get a good second-in-command. But more is not what drives most second-in-commands. People like me want a good lifestyle, we want to be shown appreciation and respect, and finally, we need to reevaluate our value frequently. Jim, you do these things well, and that is why I'm so happy here."

Brett's statement gave Jim a slight sense of relief.

He continued with confidence. "If I can be so bold, can I give you a few ideas of how to almost guarantee my long-term commitment?"

Jim was all ears, sitting with a pen over the paper, ready to write. "Absolutely. Brett. This is important to both of us."

"Okay, here goes." Brett walked over to the white board in Jim's office and began to write. "First item would be recognition. I hate to ask for this because nobody wants to have to ask for it. But I'm no different from anyone else. I, as do most people, like to be told I did a good job. For me it's really about confidence. When you tell me I've done well it gives me confidence to continue my efforts and to look for more areas where I can contribute. I can promise you that every time you've given me private or public recognition, I've brought new energy and more results soon after. This is a great strength of yours, Jim. You've never been short of letting me know the impact I'm making on this company.

"The second item I would suggest is annual compensation discussions. You can't imagine the pressure I receive from the outside world on my value. I don't mean to scare you, but since my first job as a second-in-command, I have had monthly offers from clients, vendors, friends, and miscellaneous businesses. A second-in-command won't last very long if they jump around to every offer that comes their way, but some offers can get pretty attractive at times.

"But money is absolutely not the driver of a second-in-command's decision to work somewhere. It is more of a way to keep score. It is something that should be looked at every six months to check the value. Market value and return on investment should be considered. I'm not saying I should get a raise every six months. I'd even be willing to take pay decreases every once in a while if it's best for the business. But the discussion around my value would make it easier to say no thanks to the outside world because we would be in agreement about what's fair for both of us. Again, you have treated me fairly in this area, and our annual discussions have been fair and very collaborative. I have no complaints, but the every-six-month discussions could give us both a better way of understanding and creating value."

Brett continued, "The third suggestion would be to define perpetuation strategies as soon as possible in the relationship. A first-in-command wouldn't want to offer something to a second-in-command too soon. But a structure of a deal should be introduced early, and as soon as the confidence is in place, a deal should be finalized. You gave me clarity on what our perpetuation opportunities look like, and I've agreed to that plan. I think we're on a great path in this area as well. Finally, and probably most important of all, is communication."

This caught Jim's attention because he thought one of the biggest things they had talked about on the retreat was communication, and they had a perfectly good strategy in place. He wondered what Brett was implying. "Brett, I thought we had a great communication model. What is it that we need to do about communication?"

Brett understood why Jim would be shocked by his comment. "Sorry, Jim; I didn't mean to insinuate our communication strategy needed to be changed. I was talking to my brother-in-law the other day, and he was telling me how he was struggling with his business partner because of a problem with perceived fairness. I asked him if he had addressed it with his partner. The answer shocked me. He said that he couldn't talk to his partner about something like that because they didn't trust each other that much. I was shocked, but as I thought about it, I could see how not having good rules for the game between partners could end up that way.

"I want to make sure we don't ever get in that position. I want to have a communication agreement. I would like to set a rule between us that allows either of us to go to the other in the event we feel like we're not being treated fairly. We have to have the freedom to say what's on our minds and trust that we will do the right things by and for each other."

Jim liked this a lot because it was his nature to be honest and address issues. He felt it was unfair to be held responsible to fix something he didn't know existed. "Absolutely, Brett! I think this is a great strategy. On a scale of one to ten, how would you say we're are doing in this area today?"

Brett could see that his pragmatic style was pushing Jim a little right now. He didn't want that perception. "Jim, I couldn't be happier and would say we're at a ten. That's why the whole first- and second-in-command thing is working so well for us. I don't think the noise would be gone if we had any issues in this area. I'm just glad we discussed these issues today, because these are the things that caused me to leave my prior second-in-command positions. I wouldn't want to see this happen to us. We're not only doing okay, we're doing great, and I really respect you for bringing this up. It shows that you believe in honest communication."

Jim relaxed a little after hearing these words. "Well, Brett, I can tell you that it got really noisy at lunch today during my meeting with Mike. I hadn't thought through these things, and without this discussion I might have had a lot more noise in the future. It looks to me like we've just found the final element of what it takes to really make the noise go away!"

Epilogue

THE REST OF THE STORY

T EN YEARS HAVE PASSED and the company perpetuation plan that Jim and Brett had worked so hard to prepare has come to fruition. Jim has decided to hand over the reigns of Golden Electric Supply Company to Brett. Brett will now be the President/ CEO and *first-in-command.* But that doesn't mean that Jim is going to *completely* retire. Jim has formed a new company that will consult with other businesses, passing along the principles and concepts developed by he and Brett to other executives who want to "*make their noise go away.*"

Over the past ten years, Jim and Brett have brought Golden Electric Supply to new heights. The company expanded into a new location on the east side of Denver in Commerce City. The expansion was expedited by the acquisition of another electric supply company that had closed its doors due to the death of its founder. Without a business succession plan the business was forced to close and they were able to acquire the business and inventory at wholesale prices.

The company has enjoyed financial and market success. Awards for "*Best Small Business of the Year,*" and "*Best Company to Work For*" were just some of the accolades bestowed on the company. Suppliers have provided Golden with special offers and discounts just to get their products on Golden's shelves. Life was good.

Jim has been providing the consulting advice for a few years now. He has decided to work with a very targeted type of client.

The knowledge and wisdom gained over the years at Golden and his experiences with his second-in-command have taught him to look for certain characteristics in leadership that are amenable to these valuable concepts.

Jim is careful to screen potential clients to determine if they possess the necessary traits that would allow them to accept the key principles that make the noise to go away. He interviews the first-in-command to see if he or she has the basic skill-sets, proper attitude, motivation, business acumen, industry knowledge, and above all the willingness to change old habits and beliefs.

Jim's first priorities now are his family, the cabin, and of course trout fishing. He is exactly where he hoped he would be at this time in his life and he's enjoying every minute of it. He will continue to check in with Brett from time to time, as they still have a close personal relationship that has matured and solidified with time.

Now that Jim is handing over the reins to Brett, they realized the first priority was to find an effective second-in-command. They started the search a few months before Brett took over the job of President.

Susan Edwards had all the right credentials and work experience, and the second-in-command hiring process gave them great confidence they had the right person. Prior to coming on board they gave her Brett's book, *Make the Noise Go Away*, so she could be prepared for the new relationship she would have with Brett.

Brett felt the best way to orient Susan into the new position would be to go on a retreat similar to what he and Jim took ten years earlier. Brett invited Susan and her husband to go up to Jim's mountain home with their families for a weekend of work and fun. The objective would be to get to know each other better and have Jim and Brett go over the principles of making the noise go away.

They arrived early Saturday morning and Susan's husband, Mike, was off to try his hand at fly fishing, just as Brett had promised as a way of enticing him to come along on this outing. Brett didn't think it fair that Mike had to suffer through all this business talk and had convinced both Susan and Mike that the fishing was too good to pass up.

Before the business discussions were to begin, Jim, Brett and Susan walked out onto the porch to take in the beauty of the surroundings and breathe in the fresh mountain air. It was a nostalgic moment for Brett and Jim. Things had changed a lot over the past ten years but the view and the experience of walking on the deck together was the same as ten years earlier.

While Jim and Brett were preparing the flip chart to discuss the concepts of how to *Make the Noise Go Away*, Susan looked over the balcony taking in the beauty of the mountains. She turned to the two men and expressed her feelings in the moment, *"Wow, it sure is quiet up here!"* Jim and Brett turned to each other and broke into uncontrollable laughter ...

Made in the USA
San Bernardino, CA
01 November 2014